Praise for *How to Be an Inclusive Leader*

"Though most leaders possess the desire to have more inclusive organizations, many quietly struggle with the challenge of not knowing how. Jennifer Brown's *How to Be an Inclusive Leader* gives courageous and compassionate executives a simple yet powerful blueprint for how to create true belonging and a culture where everyone can thrive. I highly recommend this book."
—**Rha Goddess, founder and CEO, Move the Crowd, and author of** *The Calling*

"Jennifer and I have a shared purpose in inspiring people to become the inclusive leaders our world needs. This book brings that purpose to life in a necessary read—an intuitive, accessible road map that will inspire you to step up, put your voice into action, and discover how to play a part in building inclusive organizations for all."
—**Torin Perez, TED Resident and author of** *Who Am I to Lead?*

"With this important contribution, Jennifer Brown invites readers to see themselves in the inclusion conversation and in the solution. *How to Be an Inclusive Leader* provides a road map to step into conversations, however imperfectly, and to learn to take action—and ultimately become someone others would consider an ally or advocate."
—**Michael Skolnik, cofounder of The Soze Agency**

"From subconscious biases that affect hiring decisions to systemic blind spots that perpetuate unequal advancement opportunities, the modern workforce is rife with inequalities. *How to Be an Inclusive Leader* is all about deepening your awareness so you can be a part of the solution. Jennifer is giving the call to action we all need!"
—**Adam Pisoni, founder and CEO, Abl Schools**

"This is the essential book so many people have been asking for. A clear how-to guide that meets leaders where they are and helps them move forward as inclusive leaders. Jennifer Brown guides us with grace and candor through her easy-to-understand framework of becoming an inclusive leader. Whether you have long been part of this conversation or are just joining it, this book has much to offer."
—**Dolly Chugh, Associate Professor, NYU Stern School of Business, and author of**
   The Person You Mean to Be

"Sometimes it seems like inequality is a massive, unfixable problem. This book shows that isn't true. Every single person can take simple steps to make his or her organization a more welcoming, inclusive environment where everyone can thrive. This book is an exceptional resource for the modern leader!"
—**Aaron Hurst, cofounder and CEO, Imperative, author of** *The Purpose Economy*
   and *Fast Company***'s Purposeful CEO series, and founder of Taproot Foundation**

"Jennifer's book is a must-read for anyone passionate about excelling in the art of inclusion."

—**Tina Alexis Allen, actress and author of *Hiding Out***

"To feel joy at work and do good work, we need to be ourselves and be appreciated for the talent we bring. Yet it's not easy to create an inclusive workplace without the skill and information we need to do that. Jennifer Brown's book provides that resource to enable us, as employers, to transform our workplace into one in which all employees feel that they belong."

—**Louise Chernin, President and CEO, GSBA, Washington State's LGBTQ Chamber of Commerce**

"Creating a culture of belonging requires each of us to harness our ability, and our responsibility, to ensure others are welcomed, valued, respected, and heard. With this book, Jennifer is empowering each of us with the tools to effect meaningful change in our workplaces."

—**Kimberley Messer, Global Diversity Business Development Leader, North America, IBM**

"With *How to Be an Inclusive Leader*, Jennifer Brown clearly shares what any individual can do to leverage one's privilege on behalf of those who may not yet have an influential voice, as well as help shape the solutions. It's ultimately about becoming a leader—a meaningful ally and equality advocate for all."

—**Monica L. Boll, Managing Director and Operations Account Executive, Accenture**

"Wow! Jennifer Brown really gets it. Her book *How to Be an Inclusive Leader* is a smart, moving, and—best of all—convincing manual for how to become the inclusive leaders we so desperately need. Her sage advice is perfect for all leaders, regardless of where they're starting on the path to becoming aware of privilege and bias and no matter the industry. This is one heck of a human book that really just might change the world."

—**Erica Keswin, founder of the Spaghetti Project and author of *Bring Your Human to Work***

"Jennifer takes a tricky and nuanced subject and makes it accessible and encouraging. I love how she gives the tools needed to create change from both an individual and organizational level, using compelling examples across industries."

—**Claire Wasserman, founder and CEO, Ladies Get Paid**

HOW TO BE AN
INCLUSIVE
LEADER

HOW TO BE AN
INCLUSIVE
LEADER

Your Role in Creating Cultures of
Belonging Where Everyone Can Thrive

JENNIFER BROWN

Berrett–Koehler Publishers, Inc.

Berrett-Koehler Publishers, Inc.
1333 Broadway, Suite 1000
Oakland, CA 94612-1921
Tel: (510) 817-2277
Fax: (510) 817-2278
www.bkconnection.com

ORDERING INFORMATION

Quantity sales. Special discounts are available on quantity purchases by corporations, associations, and others. For details, contact the "Special Sales Department" at the Berrett-Koehler address above.

Individual sales. Berrett-Koehler publications are available through most bookstores. They can also be ordered directly from Berrett-Koehler: Tel: (800) 929-2929; Fax: (802) 864-7626; www.bkconnection.com.

Orders for college textbook / course adoption use. Please contact Berrett-Koehler: Tel: (800) 929-2929; Fax: (802) 864-7626.

Distributed to the U.S. trade and internationally by Penguin Random House Publisher Services.

Berrett-Koehler and the BK logo are registered trademarks of Berrett-Koehler Publishers, Inc.

Printed in the United States of America

Berrett-Koehler books are printed on long-lasting acid-free paper. When it is available, we choose paper that has been manufactured by environmentally responsible processes. These may include using trees grown in sustainable forests, incorporating recycled paper, minimizing chlorine in bleaching, or recycling the energy produced at the paper mill.

Library of Congress Cataloging-in-Publication Data
  Names: Brown, Jennifer, 1971- author.
   Title: How to be an inclusive leader : your role in creating cultures of belonging where everyone can thrive / Jennifer Brown.
   Description: First Edition. | Oakland, CA : Berrett-Koehler Publishers, 2019.
   Identifiers: LCCN 2019011715 | ISBN 9781523085170 (hardback)
   Subjects: LCSH: Leadership. | Personnel management. | Work environment. |
    BISAC: BUSINESS & ECONOMICS / Human Resources & Personnel Management. |
    BUSINESS & ECONOMICS / Workplace Culture. | SOCIAL SCIENCE /
    Discrimination & Race Relations.
   Classification: LCC HD57.7 .B7656 2019 | DDC 658.4/092—dc23
   LC record available at https://lccn.loc.gov/2019011715

First Edition
27 26 25 24 23 22 21   10 9 8

Book producer and text designer: Maureen Forys, Happenstance Type-O-Rama
Cover designer: Dan Tesser, Studio Carnelian

Several generations of very special women have served as my pilot lights.

To Deb Ziegler, who lifted me out of despair and showed me another way to make my voice matter.

To Mimi Brown, with whom I've conspired for years on deep matters of the soul.

And most importantly, to my partner Michelle whose activist spirit and companionship I take respite in, every day of our lives together.

Contents

Preface

When I was thinking about the title for this book, including the word *how* seemed crucial. As a diversity and inclusion consultant and speaker, the question I get asked most often from audiences who are craving guidance, direction, and ideas is, "How can I improve and how do I start?"

Focusing on *how* inspired me to write this book. Ample literature out there focuses on *why*—why diversity is important, why it matters, and why leaders everywhere should cultivate cultures where people feel welcomed, supported, and driven to do their best. But, for those I know who are poised and ready to do the work that's needed, I couldn't find a clearly written, step-by-step guide that honestly laid out the pieces of the personal and emotional journey we undertake when we decide to awaken to our potential to be more inclusive.

After more than ten years of working directly with leaders in a range of industries, I've observed firsthand that understanding *how* to embark on this journey is the single most important factor when it comes to making real progress on inclusion. Although some of us embody a mindset in which we're constantly immersed in thoughts of fairness, privilege, equality, and advocacy, others are only vaguely aware of these topics on a daily basis—or are not aware of them at all. No matter where we start, as leaders, we all have a responsibility to learn how to improve our knowledge, skills, and competencies to better support our colleagues, companies, and the people around us.

> *No matter where we start, as leaders, we have a responsibility.*

Based on many years of watching all kinds of people react to the issues surrounding diversity, equity, inclusion, and belonging, my team and I developed what I call the *Inclusive Leader Continuum*, a four-step journey that codifies a set of easy-to-remember developmental stages. This book describes each of the four stages in the continuum and shows how leaders can begin to think differently, gain new perspectives, and take meaningful action to make a bigger impact in each stage. No matter your title or how advanced you already consider yourself to be as an inclusive leader, this book will lay out simple steps to help you evolve, understand your role, take action, boost your self-awareness, and become a better version of yourself in the process.

As someone with a foot in several worlds of identity-based disadvantages as well as privileges, for decades I have personally been on my own journey of endeavoring to feel seen, heard, and valued.

My earlier years as a professional were about wrestling with what it meant to be underrepresented, or simply invisible, in the workplace as a member of the LGBTQ+ (lesbian, gay, bisexual, transgender, and queer or questioning) community. I came out when I was twenty-two and struggled to find examples of professionals who were like me in the roles I aspired to fill one day. Very few women, and even fewer openly gay professionals, seemed to be at the top. Feeling like the other in the workplace often dominated my thoughts. I had a pervasive fear that, if people knew the real me, they would like me less or even view me with disdain. So, for a long time, I hid the parts of me that I feared would be rejected. I avoided sharing personal stories; I didn't even talk about what I did on weekends. Eventually, the weight of covering up who I really was felt too heavy to bear. I decided that ripping off the proverbial Band-Aid would be best for me. One day, I marched into my boss's office with a picture of my partner, Michelle, thrust it in front of him and blurted out, "I want you to know about this person who is so important to me." I paused, holding my breath. My boss looked surprised for a moment. Then he smiled and asked me to tell him all about Michelle. I was so relieved to come out of that dark, dark closet.

What's interesting is that, in many ways, people view me as the kind of person unlikely to struggle with inequality. I am Caucasian, able-bodied, and was raised in a world of privilege. I grew up in a safe home where I didn't want for anything and where I was told I could be anything I wanted. And yet I still felt like an outsider at work, which seemed like a major disadvantage when it came to me progressing up the career ladder. It made me think about how many other people feel the same way, for a whole range of reasons, some hidden underneath the surface, but some most certainly not. If I could hide the parts of myself that didn't appear to be valued or even accepted, then what about those who don't have the same option—to hide things and who must regularly face indirect, subtle, or overt discrimination because of who they are?

We all have such different experiences in life—certain advantages and disadvantages. But what if, instead of hiding our truths, we could bring our *full* selves to work—without it feeling like a liability—and empower others to do the same? This question has been a driving force for me since I first entered the workforce, and it was a major factor in my decision to start my own business. I wanted to use my experiences and passion for advocacy to help organizations create cultures of belonging where everyone can thrive and contribute to their fullest potential. Today, my team and I advise Fortune 500s and many others on how to build more inclusive workplaces in which all kinds of talent can feel welcomed, valued, respected, and heard. This is especially poignant because I used to be that voiceless employee who was hiding, not bringing my full self to work, and not able to align myself with my organization's mission because I never knew for certain whether or not I was a valued part of the workforce.

The hard truth is that, with a labor market that's becoming more and more competitive, and with a workforce that has grown increasingly diverse, leaders who aren't making an effort to become more inclusive are at growing risk of falling behind. Not being able to draw the best out of your people or attract and retain top talent can be disastrous for business. I've seen this play out in organizations all over the world. The root causes are almost always a lack of understanding from leadership when it comes to what the issues are, and what role they should play in resolving those issues, and a lack of managerial courage to take action and step into advocacy for *all* of their workforce, current and future.

> *Not being able to draw the best*
> *out of your people or attract*
> *and retain top talent can be*
> *disastrous for business.*

No matter whether you already consider yourself an advocate for diversifying the teams, communities, and workplaces in your life, or are just starting to consider how some of the people around you might have a tougher climb up the ladder, this book will meet you where you are and show you how you can begin to become more inclusive.

The good news is, there isn't a wrong starting point if your intent is to grow. I welcome you and commit that, in this book, you won't be shamed; rather, you'll be awakened, equipped, and inspired by the knowledge that you are needed, that your voice can make a difference, and that taking a single step is a great and honorable place to start.

As we learn how to generate an experience of belonging for others, the surprising benefit is that we often discover and begin to understand those parts of ourselves that we (or our organizations or, indeed, society at large) have negated, marginalized, or denied. We can revisit our own stories of exclusion and examine where our voice gets lost, isn't heard, or where we aren't showing courage in authenticity. Exclusion is a universally understood feeling and, when we finally embrace all our human experiences, we realize we each have plenty to work with; instead of our lives having throwaway or irrelevant details, we discover we have wisdom to share. This book will empower you to activate from this deeply personal place so that you can go on to become a true instrument of change.

Introduction
From Unaware to Advocate

'm in a conference room with twenty-five white male executives. Every face I look at is either scowling at me or watching the clock. I'm certain none of them wants to be here. As I start to speak, I notice my palms are sweating.

I'm here to talk about inclusion and why it matters. It's not the first time I've spoken to the Fortune 500 about this subject, but this particular company has been in the headlines lately, in a very unflattering light. Homophobic and sexist comments were made on the trading floor and a harassment suit followed. The CEO is not okay with what transpired, so he hired my team to gather employee reactions and find out how this happened. Today I am here to deliver some not-so-great feedback. Unfortunately, the CEO is not attending the meeting. This, in itself, may be sending a message that the issues they are up against aren't truly a priority.

In rooms like this, while I'm not in any physical danger, I still don't feel safe. I'm on high alert before I say a word. I scan the room and confirm that, from what I can observe, I'm the only woman present. It's a familiar feeling, but I'm reminded again, in this moment, of the lower status of my gender in the business world. I wonder if they've already written me off and how I can overcome this automatic dismissal. Although I can't be certain, I suspect that I'm also the only person in the room who identifies as a member of the LGBTQ+ community. I'm positive my sexual orientation hasn't crossed their minds because, in many ways, I defy the stereotype that others hold about how someone thus identified "should" look.

As I begin to facilitate the conversation, I'm also calculating: How brave am I feeling? To what extent have I personally experienced what I'm reporting, and should I share that? Does doing so strengthen, weaken, or distract from my argument? Will I have less credibility, in their minds, if I align myself and my personal experiences with those experiencing exclusion, and even harassment? I sense my success with this group will be determined by my ability to detach and appear objective. I present the data in a dispassionate, clinical way so that no one can accuse me of positive bias toward certain identities. This is necessary because I suspect I am already only holding their attention by a thread.

Strong opinions are part of every executive discussion, and today is no exception. Several loud voices dominate the conversation, question the data, and minimize the feedback I share. They back each other up, building on each other's points, and the momentum of resistance increases. Deflections fill the room (and these are just the ones that are verbalized):

"I don't want to know about people's personal challenges."

"People need to stop being so sensitive."

"I don't care if you're black, white, or purple—I hire the best person for the job."

And the inevitable "Are you suggesting we should have quotas?"

After hearing what they have to say, I decide that I made the best decision by carefully leaving much of myself out of the conversation. I continue with the session, sharing the messages the CEO hired me to share, but it's hard to feel like my words might be sinking in when so many in the room aren't open to change. They have invested heavily in my being there and yet spend all of their time with me, the expert, shooting holes in the research and data (from my firm and other, much larger research institutions), and in their own employees' first-hand, self-reported experiences. I leave feeling diminished, discouraged, and unsure how many of those leaders would support me if we were working together directly. If I worked for that company, I would have serious doubts about my ability—and desire—to stay.

This experience is being repeated across workforces everywhere, every day, and I believe it's a key factor in the difficulties that organizations are facing in retaining talent. Who wants to go through this exhausting ritual, day after day? Many companies talk about making diversity, equity, and inclusion a priority but are continuing to fail in building cultures where employees of *all* demographics have a real chance to thrive.

I wrote this book to change that.

The Power of Being Inclusive

What Does It Mean?

Inclusiveness starts with a spark to do better. That spark lives inside leaders, almost like a pilot light. It's always there, ready and waiting to create a bigger flame. Leaders can create a culture of belonging where everyone can thrive in countless ways, and this book covers myriad examples. But all of those actions start with a spark—a desire or drive to evoke change. When you have that spark, you start to see all the opportunities to better support others unfold. You want to *do* more. To fulfill your potential as a leader, colleague, community member, parent, or friend. To learn, to grow, and to contribute.

The hardest part about becoming an inclusive leader can be that initial work to switch the pilot light on, to become aware that you are already equipped with the ability to make a difference and to learn how much your efforts are needed. It can be a total shift in mindset, not unlike a spiritual awakening. Having that internal flame can create a greater sense of purpose, enriching life in wonderfully unexpected ways—for yourself *and* others.

You are already equipped with the
ability to make a difference.

But to truly ignite that power, you must look inside yourself to uncover your blind spots, prejudices, and biases and overcome them. It's a humbling journey of discovery that's not always easy. Leadership is not leadership unless it's uncomfortable. If you aren't pushing yourself to do more, and pushing others around you to improve, chances are, you aren't doing enough.

Of course, this necessary discomfort is an indelible hallmark of leadership, of any kind. Often, not only are those who are considered inclusive leaders also considered great leaders in the traditional sense, but they lead with an additional vigilance, care, and intention: to perceive and then address what might be getting in the way for others around them. They are dedicated to the thriving of others, particularly those who have struggled proportionally more to be heard and valued. They honor and value input, nurture purpose in others, and encourage authenticity for those who fear the repercussions of being authentic. They are passionate about challenging whatever obstacles to potential and performance they can, and they constantly seek to learn more about what they *don't* know when it comes to cultural competency so that they can better resonate across difference and maintain trust. And they don't pursue any of this as a chore, but with enthusiasm and joy.

They take a strong stand against bias, even its most subtle forms. They understand where and when they can step in and use their voice to address bias when it occurs, they think about the systemic reasons for it occurring, and they endeavor to tackle those reasons at the root.

Inclusive leaders bring more of themselves to the workplace than other leaders, believing that through their own vulnerability and authenticity, they can create a space in which others can do the same. They don't just push others to be blindly authentic but plan with them to stretch forward, to take calculated risks, while never encouraging someone to push themselves out there before they're ready or put themselves into career peril. They always offer to be present, alongside others, to lend a voice.

They seek as much feedback as they give.

They are aware of, and know how to utilize, their privilege to raise issues, to challenge norms and behaviors, and to root out and prioritize core issues that perpetuate exclusionary dynamics.

They push themselves as much as they push others.

And they do all of this consistently.

Why Does It Matter?

Many talented employees in organizations all over the world tell us through focus groups that they don't feel comfortable bringing their whole selves to work. They are just getting by every day, and they are leaving their true talents and deepest passions elsewhere. In any organization where this is true, you can bet the bottom line is affected.

When people are actively hiding their deepest truths, gifts, unique insights, struggles, and experiences, they aren't able to fully leverage those same things for their success. Not only does this struggle to fit in lead to diminished performance, but it also saps extra energy that would be better spent working toward helping the company remain nimble and competitive.

The importance of cultivating an inclusive environment where everyone can thrive is only increasing as the world's workforce demographics continue to change. By 2020, Millennials will be more than 50 percent of the workforce. This generation and the generation after them, Generation Z, have little patience for those organizations that don't value diversity. They expect inclusive workplaces. To focus on just two characteristics, they are much more ethnically and racially diverse than previous generations. For example, American Baby Boomers are 75 percent white whereas Millennials are 55.8 percent white. And quite a few states have significantly more racially diverse populations of Millennials, such as California, where less than one third of Millennials are white.[1] With these rapidly shifting demographics, all leaders should take notice of the change on the horizon. When companies and leaders fail to cultivate inclusive environments, employees will vote with their feet, leaving to seek better options where they will be embraced.

With all this in mind, it's perhaps not surprising that two thirds of executives consider diversity and inclusion a rising priority.[2] But that may not solely be due to the negative repercussions that can occur when you don't prioritize inclusion; there are also many inspiring statistics that *support* inclusion in the workplace. For example, when companies chose to promote their female employees to top management teams between 1992 and 2006, they generated an average of one percent more economic value, which typically translated to over $40 million.[3] Similarly, Fortune 500 companies with at least three directors who are women have seen their return on invested capital increase by at least 66 percent and their sales increase by 42 percent.[4] And that's just diversity in gender for high-level leaders.

When companies improve their inclusion of other groups, the results are similarly impressive.

For instance, organizations that embrace best practices for employing and supporting more individuals with diverse abilities in their workforce have achieved 28 percent higher revenue, doubled their net income, and earned 30 percent higher profit margins than their peers. (As a leader, you might be interested to know that people of diverse abilities are an untapped talent pool of 10.7 million people.)[5] Further, companies with the most ethnically diverse executive teams are 33 percent more likely to outperform their peers on profitability.[6]

No matter which industry you're in, being profitable matters. Leaders at every level are expected to model the behaviors and take the actions that support financial success. And, increasingly, core leadership competencies are shifting to prioritize the ability to engage and retain diverse talent, with a focus on making them feel included and supported. The importance of these soft skills has been underestimated in the past, but the world is changing rapidly and leaders need to adapt as these become hard skills that will increasingly be expected, measured, and compensated accordingly.

Your Role

All of the aforementioned data shows we have much at stake in making our workplaces more inclusive and that we need to make a serious course correction. We have the opportunity to build a different future, a better future. We can choose to jump into the river and start swimming, but many of us are lingering on the shore. And yet all of us are needed—to chip in, to contribute, to get involved—not just on paper, registering our good intentions, but doing the actual work of change, especially *within* ourselves, and following a learning path with discipline and commitment. This book provides a structure for that important path as well as ideas for action steps to take at each stage.

Anyone can (and should) be an inclusive leader. Whether you're a powerful CEO or a brand-new employee who doesn't have any direct reports yet, you can incorporate behaviors and actions into your routine that will help drastically change the day-to-day reality for many of your coworkers. The same is true about your current level of advancement on the topic of inclusion. Whether you consider yourself an advocate or are just dipping a toe in the water and beginning to learn what you don't know, you're in the right place. I wrote this book to equip leaders everywhere who have ever felt uncertain about their next steps when it comes to inclusion with a proven step-by-step process they can put to work right away.

I've always admired Martin Luther King, Jr., and his confidence that the world would become a better—more just—place for us all. I have long considered his words, "the arc of the moral universe is long, but it bends towards justice," as my guiding star, particularly when the tenets of inclusion are being challenged everywhere we look. His words give me hope when I wonder—as others did, then—"How long will it take?" His words assure me that my advocacy is not in vain. But most of all, I don't believe his words condone passivity or inaction, for any of us—or that we are all swept up in a larger momentum over which we have no control. We can't sit back and wait for the arc of history to bend by itself, believing that we are somehow inconsequential, or that we can't have an impact, or that our voices don't matter. And we can't hope for more opportunities, for *all* kinds of talent, to magically appear on their own. We have to do our part, and we still have a long way to go.

If we want a more just world, one in which more vulnerable people are spoken for and supported to succeed and in which the playing field begins to equalize, we need to grasp the urgency of our *own* role and responsibility to bend that arc.

A New Theory of Change: The Inclusive Leader Continuum

After working with countless teams on diversity and inclusion, I started noticing commonalities in leaders' perspectives and learning patterns. The people who were just beginning to understand the importance of inclusion had similar struggles and opportunities. Similarly, the people at the other end of the spectrum—those who had dedicated their careers to becoming advocates for those who are less represented (including themselves, in some cases) also had their own set of struggles and opportunities. Because I had gotten to know so many people on their journey to becoming more inclusive leaders, it seemed natural to develop a multistage model for learners to use to identify their current state—in terms of knowledge and mindset—and most importantly, to anticipate next steps and develop goals for progress *toward* something. As human beings, we need to have at least a sense of what we're shooting for. We may all agree that inclusion seems important, and that we want to be inclusive leaders; each stage in this book makes visible the journey to get there, with its own learning points, opportunities for growth, and actions that will help you start building or activating the muscles that will ultimately help you advance to the next level.

The stages of the Inclusive Leader Continuum, which illustrate how anyone can begin to shift their thinking, gain new perspectives, use their voice, and take meaningful action to create cultures of belonging, are as follows:

UNAWARE When you are in this stage, you don't notice or understand that certain demographic groups, or those with specific backgrounds and experiences, have a much harder time thriving at work. You think diversity is compliance related and simply tolerate it. In this stage, people are disengaged from the conversation around diversity and inclusion and/or uninterested in it. This resistance may be silent or public.

AWARE You realize the playing field is not level in the workplace or in other group or organizational contexts and that you have been blind in some ways when it comes to inclusion. This stage is about beginning to understand other people's perspectives and stories and working through your own stories and biases.

ACTIVE You are proactively working toward equity and equal opportunities, supporting those with underrepresented or marginalized identities, backgrounds, and experiences. This stage is about pushing outside of your comfort zone, building new muscles, and finding your voice as your inclusive actions become more visible and you shift your priorities.

ADVOCATE You are becoming a voice that is capable of transforming biased systems and sparking meaningful, widespread, and scalable lasting change. This stage is hallmarked by brave public actions that challenge deeply rooted beliefs and practices and taking some calculated personal or professional risk to shift behaviors.

We all currently reside somewhere among these stages when it comes to our general mindset and daily actions, and there are no judgments about where you find yourself today. Some inclusive leaders bloom late in life into the desire to change and grow—maybe thanks to a single point in time or an aha moment, or a series of realizations over time—while others grow up already more attuned to the world around them and the part they have to play. Whether your journey ignites with one moment or takes many years, it begins with a series of important steps.

In addition to residing in one of these stages for our mindset, we revisit each of these stages over and over again when we learn about demographics and experiences that are new to us. For example, even though it's my job to know about diversity and I'm a woman and a member of the LGBTQ+ community, I don't begin to assume advocate-level knowledge of all unique groups of people in the world. So when I broaden my knowledge on, say, military veterans' unique challenges and opportunities when they reenter the civilian workforce, I start back at the beginning of the continuum and make my way forward.

You will have the same experience with the continuum. It's not a linear journey that we travel only once. We travel forward and backwards many times as we learn, make mistakes, and grow. All of this is to be expected. It can help to think of your growth toward becoming an inclusive leader as being like a new habit you want to build, and then grow comfortable with being a bit (or very) uncomfortable along the way.

Visit inclusiveleaderthebook.com to take the How to Be an Inclusive Leader assessment and discover where you currently reside on the continuum, as well as which steps you need to take next in order to move forward.

During this journey, it's essential that we don't become critical of ourselves or others or place judgment based on where people are in the continuum. Instead, let's focus on making progress. Everyone who reads this book will be starting from a different place, and we all have a great deal to learn at every stage. That's why I recommend reading through each stage in this book, which I've organized into individual chapters, no matter where you think your starting point might be today.

Think of your inclusive leader journey as an investment in yourself and your career stock, no matter what your level in your organization. It is my strong prediction, which is backed up by multiple research and thought leadership organizations, that the mindset and skills needed to be an inclusive leader will be top of mind in nearly every organization as we move deeper into the twenty-first century. Not only is the topic frequently in our headlines with so many institutions grappling with a lack of diversity and so many big names being toppled after they misused their power and privilege, but many organizations are in a panic about recruiting and retaining the best talent from all kinds of backgrounds, because they know their cultures are not supportive of all newcomers and they struggle even with retaining their current employees. As a leader who understands and supports inclusion, you will have the right kind of skills to get the most out of your team, at the very least maintaining your job security through times of great disruption, but I anticipate and am confident that you will discover much more.

Glossary: *Part of being an inclusive leader is understanding key words and concepts, and being able to incorporate this language into your vernacular. I included a glossary in the back of the book to define keywords and concepts. From Chapter One forward, I put these terms in* **bold** *when I first mention them in the book (with the exception of the different stages of the continuum, which are discussed in detail in this first chapter), and I often provide a short explanation or story to help illustrate their meaning. If you come across a term again later in the book and you want a refresher on the meaning, you can flip to the Glossary and look it up.*

If You Can Get Them, Can You Keep Them?

Forward-thinking leaders know that diversity in their workforce translates into an enhanced ability to build better, more innovative products and services, as well as attract the best and brightest teams. But they also know that hiring certain percentages of diverse talent won't solve all their problems. Bringing more nontraditional candidates in is not the same as being able to keep them, particularly over time; bias still permeates organizations and affects certain employees more profoundly. All talent needs to be supported properly along their career journey or they won't thrive, and this is most true for talent who don't see many, or any, who look like them at the leadership levels. This is a key reason why widespread corporate diversity and inclusion efforts have not resulted in much representational change at the top of organizations. For instance, as I write this only three Fortune 500 CEOs are people of color (the lowest figure since 2002), only one is openly gay (Apple's Tim Cook), and only 4.8 percent are women.

Arguably more attention needs to be directed toward retaining said talent by developing a culture of belonging, where everyone is included, within an organization. If inclusiveness isn't a priority, then discerning employees, only hired to fill a quota or deflect accusations of discrimination, won't thrive or stay for long. An inclusive workplace only happens when leaders agree to take a closer look at themselves, unravel their biases, and do the hard work that's necessary to bring about a fair shot for all.

Before We Embark

Over many years of supporting diversity networks in companies of all sizes, I have learned that each person is differently affected, through the lens of their particular identity, by what's happening outside the proverbial four walls of a company. As leaders, it is essential that we understand this context, because it strongly influences what we see in the workplace. I've spoken to people firsthand who don't have the luxury of being able to check that reality at the door when they come to work. These are people who are either overtly or subtly discriminated against—perhaps because of their gender, age, ethnicity, religion, disability, sexual orientation, gender identity, or socioeconomic status—and who are having a radically different experience at work than those with relatively more privilege or advantage, and they often hide these experiences beneath the surface.

Awake to uncertain tides, some are more on guard than ever, hoping to avoid conflicts with their coworkers. They are distracted, worried, and feel compelled to blend in wherever possible, rather than risk bringing their true selves to work and face being stereotyped, losing trusted relationships, missing out on upcoming promotions, or worse.

Even if inclusion is not top of mind for you, it is worth everything to other people. Compassion and empathy for others' stories and experiences starts with us. We can't outsource the work to others or delegate it to the diversity team or diversity leaders in our organizations. We all have a responsibility to act. I challenge you to humble yourself to all that you don't know and see learning as the opportunity that it is: your access to breakthrough thinking and results. The key thing is to remember to keep moving forward, however incrementally.

The Inclusive Leader Continuum

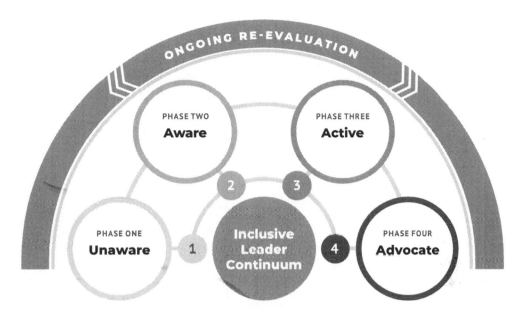

ONGOING RE-EVALUATION

PHASE TWO
Aware

PHASE THREE
Active

PHASE ONE
Unaware

Inclusive Leader Continuum

PHASE FOUR
Advocate

UNAWARE
You think diversity is compliance-related and simply tolerate it. It's someone else's job—not yours.

AWARE
You are aware that you have a role to play and are educating yourself about how best to move forward.

ACTIVE
You have shifted your priorities and are finding your voice as you begin to take meaningful action in support of others.

ADVOCATE
You are proactively and consistently confronting discrimination and working to bring about change in order to prevent it on a systemic level.

Private /// Low Risk /// Individual Perspective → Public /// High Risk /// Organizational Perspective

To support your learning journey and discover where you are currently on the Inclusive Leader Continuum, take our proprietary online assessment at inclusiveleaderthebook.com.

CHAPTER ONE

Starting Your Journey

You are empowered. If you want to get healthy, you don't wait for some-one to hand you vegetables—you get informed, you research nutrition, and you challenge yourself to start exercising! Don't wait for someone to hand you a broader worldview. Go get it.

—LESLIE SLATON BROWN, Chief Diversity Officer, Hewlett-Packard

As you begin turning pages in this book, you will find that I won't always be able to provide simple answers for dealing with complex situations. Each organization is unique, and each diversity dilemma has its own dimensions. What I *do* commit to is giving you a new framework with which to understand yourself as a key player in your company, our society, and in the wider world in this critical moment as we move toward greater and greater diversity. I am going to give you the tools to wield so you can be an active leader rather than a passive **bystander** and be someone who attempts to make positive change, rather than someone who's at the mercy of the changes happening all around them.

In my bid to simplify a complex topic, reflect what I have observed to be true, and inspire you, the reader, into action, I came up with what is the central architecture of this book—the *Inclusive Leader Continuum*. The more I share it with audiences around the world, the more confirmation I receive of its universal applicability. Everyone can find themselves in it somewhere, often at multiple points, depending on their knowledge about and level of advocacy on behalf of different communities of people.

When it comes to something as multilayered as diversity, none of us is an expert. We can always be doing something more, specifically for communities that need the support of our voice and social or professional **capital**. You will learn more about such opportunities in this book.

> *When it comes to something as multilayered as diversity, none of us is an expert. We can always be doing something more.*

The Stages of the Inclusive Leader Continuum

The Inclusive Leader Continuum has four stages, each with a few distinctive characteristics (see Figure 1.1).

Unaware

Everyone has to start somewhere, and the first stage of the journey along the continuum is hallmarked by not knowing much about the issues around inclusion or how inequalities are perpetuated. It's easy

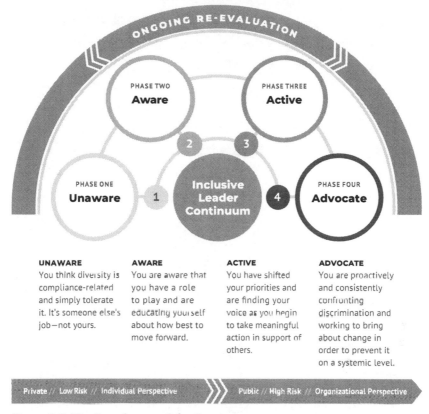

| **UNAWARE** | **AWARE** | **ACTIVE** | **ADVOCATE** |
| You think diversity is compliance-related and simply tolerate it. It's someone else's job—not yours. | You are aware that you have a role to play and are educating yourself about how best to move forward. | You have shifted your priorities and are finding your voice as you begin to take meaningful action in support of others. | You are proactively and consistently confronting discrimination and working to bring about change in order to prevent it on a systemic level. |

Private // Low Risk // Individual Perspective ⟫⟫ Public // High Risk // Organizational Perspective

Figure 1.1. The Four Stages of the Continuum

to live in this stage if you're part of a majority demographic and you grew up without being exposed to many different types of people. Inclusion might not seem like a pressing issue because you haven't really experienced the feeling of exclusion.

Many people remain at this stage because they believe they're well-intentioned and that things will just work out. They might believe in their own innate goodness and that their progressive values are obvious to other people, so they don't think they need to say or do anything differently. What they don't realize is that inequalities are so baked in to systems and processes that it takes real effort to disrupt the status quo. They also don't realize that the benefits of an inclusive workplace often need to be fought for and are worth fighting for; those benefits include better team cohesion, higher productivity and retention and, ultimately, higher profitability.

To work toward equality, many individuals must work together, including those who *haven't* felt excluded in society or the workplace. This stage is about beginning to understand the reality of inequalities in the workplace and the role every inclusive leader should play in making a difference.

Aware

At this stage, you begin to understand how much you don't know and realize you have so much left to learn. This stage is for deep self-reflection and internal dialogue about how your perceived experience does not square with others' world reality. This stage will likely require you to acknowledge your own inner discomforts and the experiences that led you to experience them. In the process, you may realize that you've been making work decisions based almost solely on your own experiences without considering other perspectives. In addition to such overwhelming realizations, this stage may also come with some shame or guilt about missed opportunities. You may come to understand your colleagues' advantages and disadvantages and what has made their lives and career progressions relatively easier or harder. These insights contain clues for action.

At this stage, you reflect on whom you've sought out for support and where you haven't felt supported, and you explore, perhaps for the first time, what kind of support you can give and who is most in need of it. This stage awakens you to your own limitations and advantages and asks that you activate in order to make changes for yourself and your workplace.

Active

What good is knowledge if it's not applied? The choice to become active is the do-or-die moment for anyone aspiring to be an inclusive leader. This is the moment when you sign up to do more, to put yourself into places of discomfort, and to assume a new level of responsibility as a friend, colleague, and especially as a leader. In this stage, you also need to shed unproductive behaviors, mindsets, and resistance points that have either prevented you from taking action in the past or that continue to distract you and slow you down.

At this stage, you're communicating ideas that are new to you and are trying to find your voice, which can feel awkward. This stage might come with more risk because you are more visibly taking action. As you start to express your own perceptions and try to be more inclusive, things won't always go smoothly. Some people won't agree with your views, and others won't like the way you communicate those views—even if your heart is in the right place. As with anything, humility and resilience are key. If you feel the sting of criticism, don't decide it's easier to watch from the sidelines. Remember, nothing worth fighting for is easy.

Advocate

Once you've exercised your fledgling skills during the Active stage, you are ready for more. Now you can focus on not just who needs support, but also how systems need to evolve to interrupt harmful practices that perpetuate an unequal playing field. In other words, you're committed in word and deed to making your workplace more inclusive.

You may find yourself increasingly ready to be more public with your efforts to be bolder, to challenge others more directly, and to question systems that so many people have taken for granted. This seemingly fearless stance becomes your new normal. You learn the language of inclusion and get comfortable with knowing you will make mistakes. Others begin to follow along and gain inspiration from you.

You can think of this stage as a natural inclination: when you see something, you say something and you do something. You speak up when you hear inappropriate language or humor. You wonder why the new intern pool isn't more diverse and suggest strategies to change it. You are used to being uncomfortable, routinely, and you can confidently use the tools at your disposal to influence others or gain their support.

I organized this book into chapters that align with this journey. Think of it as a step-by-step guide to become an inclusive leader. However, one of the most important things to remember is that *no one travels along the continuum only once.* You will travel back and forth between stages multiple times, depending on which community or identity you're currently educating yourself about. For example, you may feel confident advocating for the LGBTQ+ community as a whole but still find yourself unaware of the challenges that transgender or non-binary people face. As the saying goes, you don't know what you don't know. That's why I believe all leaders can benefit from returning again and again to the Unaware stage and working their way back through the continuum.

You are apt to find that the stories and examples in the earlier chapters will broaden your thinking and help you gain new perspectives on a range of issues. As you uncover your knowledge gaps and biases and change the way you think about supporting different groups of people, you will move on to the next stage. You may also learn how to better relate to colleagues who are at the beginning of their journeys to becoming inclusive leaders and begin to understand how you might help them advance. Rather than considering advocacy a destination, it's better to see the continuum as a journey, one on which you try to make progress every day.

Diversity Dimensions

If you've been thinking that inclusion doesn't affect you directly, think again. Most of us have both visible and invisible aspects of diversity, or so-called **diversity dimensions**. These parts of our identity make us who we are. Many people do not feel totally comfortable sharing all these parts of themselves at work, so they downplay who they are in order to belong. This is called **covering**. In a white paper entitled "Uncovering Talent," New York University School of Law Professor Kenji Yoshino and former Deloitte University Leadership Center for Inclusion Managing Principal Christie Smith identify four main categories across which many people feel the need to downplay their identities:[1]

APPEARANCE   Individuals alter their self-presentation, including grooming, attire, and mannerisms, to blend into the mainstream (for example, a Black woman might straighten her hair to deemphasize her race,[2] or a Jewish man might go to synagogue in the morning, then take his kippah off when he gets to work).

AFFILIATION   Individuals avoid behaviors widely associated with their identity in order to negate stereotypes about that identity (for example, a mother may not talk about her children in case anyone infers she is less committed to her work, or someone older than others in their position might be careful not to mention their age or anything that might date them).

ADVOCACY   Individuals avoid specific topics related to their identity so they don't have to defend that particular group (for example, a veteran might not challenge a joke about the military, or someone of Chinese descent might not correct people if they make comments that use Asian stereotypes).

ASSOCIATION Individuals avoid being around certain others (for example, an LGBTQ+ person may not bring their same-sex partner as a +1 to work functions, or someone who is not a social drinker may not attend the after-work drinks they were invited to by their manager).

According to the white paper, most employees actively downplay one or more identities at work, and those who are less represented in the workforce, particularly at leadership levels, report covering more often. When people don't feel comfortable bringing their authentic selves to work, there are serious issues for both individuals and organizations. People who are constantly covering can feel isolated and unsupported by their colleagues. Such situations aren't ones in which people do their best work or in which they choose to stay if they have other job options.

> *Most employees actively downplay one or more identities at work.*

I reveal in my keynote speeches how I've become quite good at covering, myself—expending extra energy to manage my more stigmatized identities. I first developed this skill when I came out as a member of the **LGBTQ+** community in my 20s and downplayed this deep personal truth in a series of professional roles, from stage performer to HR professional to entrepreneur. I saw no role models who shared my story (at least, who openly shared it, or who were visible to me). I eventually reached a point of professional status where I found the courage to be my authentic self—most of the time. Owning my own business played a major role in this, since I didn't feel at risk of being fired or ostracized from my own staff. But I still feel vulnerable when I consult with clients and meet prospects and sense they might hold stereotypes or biases about aspects of my identity.

I am certainly not alone in this experience. Many people are worried about being judged or discriminated against at work if they draw attention to a certain part of their identity, so they never reach the point where they feel comfortable being their whole self at work.

The Tip of the Iceberg

When my consulting company works with clients, we often use the metaphor of an iceberg to explore what it means to cover. Consider Figure 1.2, which shows an iceberg floating in water, with certain diversity dimensions visible above the water and others beneath the waterline.

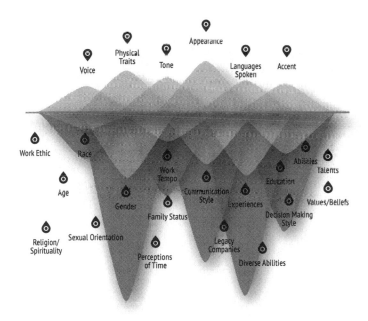

Figure 1.2. The Iceberg

Certain life experiences, like the following, can also play a huge role in our personal identity but remain invisible to our colleagues.

SOME OF THE WAYS PEOPLE COVER[3]

- I don't talk about my child who has Down Syndrome.

- I don't talk about my children and my spouse.

- I couldn't tell the executive team that I was missing important meetings to take my daughter to appointments during their transition to a man.

- I don't go out to lunch with other people because I don't want them knowing I am a diabetic.

- I go to my AA meetings during lunch and avoid events with drinks at all costs, which makes it seem like I am antisocial.

- My executive team doesn't know I have a child in prison.

- I don't share that my parents are still very poor and live in rural Appalachia.

- I don't tell people that I changed my Russian name to an American name and took classes to remove my accent.

- I take sick days to go to dialysis.

- I have to take personal days for Jewish high holidays.

- I turned down the request to lead the Disability Employee Resource Group as a sponsor because I was afraid people would find out I am bipolar.

- No one knows I have an intense fear of public speaking and I have to take medication every time I speak in front of clients.

- No one knows that I care for my father, who has HIV.

- I "pass" for white so don't keep pictures of my biracial parents at work.

- No one knows that my parents came to this country by crossing the border and that they don't speak English.

- No one knows that I am transgender.

In my company's consulting work, we meet with teams to help them understand how the iceberg metaphor plays out in people's work experiences. During our diversity workshops, we discuss the following questions:

- Which aspects of you float in plain sight for all to see?

- Which do you keep concealed beneath your waterline?

- Where do you set your waterline to feel safe?

Every one of us is so complex that it makes no sense to assume you know who someone is based on what's visible, but people make assumptions about each other nonetheless. Instead, it is immensely helpful to simply be aware that we all have an iceberg where potentially just the tip is showing.

When people meet me or work with me for the first time, they probably assume correctly that they know my race, gender, and generation, but they are likely to misidentify the less observable aspects of who I am, such as my religion, educational background, or sexual orientation. I have passing **privilege,** which means I can allow myself to be mistaken for a straight woman and choose not to bring up the fact that I have a same-sex life partner. Depending on how comfortable I am in my environment, and what behaviors or attributes are valued in my workplace, I may or may not bring up more of what has shaped my work experiences. If I do, that effectively lowers the waterline of my personal diversity iceberg.

Many others carry certain identities and are extremely familiar with this balancing act. National Public Radio began a program within the last few years using a term from linguistics as its title: *Code*

Switch. Linguists typically use **code switching** to mean the instant and frequent switching between two distinct languages, like Spanish and English among many Puerto Rican New Yorkers. But journalist Gene Demby, lead blogger for NPR's *Code Switch* team, says many of us subtly, reflexively change the way we express ourselves all the time. "We're hop-scotching between different cultural and linguistic spaces and different parts of our own identities—sometimes within a single interaction."[4]

Yoshino and Smith's research on covering in the workplace and Demby's explanation of code switching have illuminated the extent to which many individuals feel they don't belong in the workplace. They have internalized messages of exclusion and feel forced to cover and code switch in order to be included.

In exploring your role in this dynamic, you may discover that you are also covering, and that this is affecting your potential. Of course, you don't need to share all the details of your private life at work, but if you anticipate being negatively stereotyped about a certain aspect of your identity, it takes extra effort to adjust how you show up, and this valuable energy could be leaking away from your productivity.

When I'm conducting diversity workshops, I challenge executive leaders in particular to share more of who they are—to get vulnerable. It is especially critical for leaders to do this because thousands of eyes are on them and many decisions about authenticity and bringing one's full self to work can have an impact on whether or not an individual employee, looking upward, sees their story and their background reflected. In one of my workshops, a leader responded to the challenge to stop covering by "coming out" as Jewish to his Christian management team. In another workshop, an executive shared that he didn't have a college degree. Yet another shared that he'd grown up in an abusive and alcoholic family. In an age in which particularly younger talent isn't going to be persuaded to follow senior leaders based on title alone, it behooves every leader to revisit where they set the waterline on their personal iceberg and to show up more fully and honestly as human beings.

As you work to transform yourself into an inclusive leader, remember that we all know something about diversity through our own experiences, and people around us are covering on a daily basis. When a significant number of people in an organization are not reaching their full potential because they don't feel like they belong or can bring their whole selves to work, everyone is affected.

The Road Ahead

We're at a point in history in which people are increasingly ready to live their truth, both in their personal lives and at work. The myopic leadership and talent management norms that worked in the past will not keep working in the future. The dialogue about the importance of inclusion in our workplaces is accelerating, and people are finding their voices and learning how to use them. Any leader out of step with these developments, who has little curiosity about or commitment to standing up for this conversation, risks their reputation, their credibility, and most importantly, their opportunity to resonate with coworkers in a way that unleashes creativity and results. Companies that have not been prioritizing inclusion won't be able to stay competitive moving forward.

I have talked with thousands of leaders who want to be more inclusive in how they value everyone's voices at the table so they can hear diverse perspectives offered up by those voices. Like it or not, the work begins with you rolling up your sleeves and taking a long, hard look at yourself—your biases, what you say or don't say, how you might resist taking action by deflecting responsibility—before determining how you can do better and how your entire organization might do better. It also requires that you honestly assess how you show up at work—especially if you have ever felt a compulsion to downplay who you really are in order to belong.

Fortunately, in my work with so many well-meaning leaders, I have noticed a consistent pattern in their journeys from uncertainty to confidence. You can follow a well-trodden path from trepidation to transformational leadership to become the true champion of progress you have always wanted to be. By deciding to read this book, you have demonstrated that you are committed to growth, to pushing yourself, to being uncomfortable with your own limitations and inadequacies, and to opening yourself to the experiences of others— even if there is no fast track to success. And this is the best possible place from which to start your journey as an inclusive leader.

So, let us begin.

CHAPTER TWO

Unaware

Rather than think in terms of good and bad, it is more helpful to think in terms of conscious and unconscious, aware and unaware.

—JOAN BORYSENKO

In early 2018, an eleven-minute video of acclaimed motivational speaker Tony Robbins went viral. In it, a female participant at one of his conferences challenged his seeming dismissal of the #MeToo movement after he said women who share stories of sexual harassment or sexual assault are trying to gain significance by attacking and destroying someone else. In the video, which was shared thousands of times online, you can see the participant standing up in the audience as Robbins approaches her. Towering over her (he is six feet, seven inches tall), he lays a hand on her shoulder, appearing to push her backward as he explains and defends his point.

The online reaction to the content and the **optics** of this was swift. Soon after, his organization reached out to Tarana Burke, creator of the original Me Too movement in 2006 (it would be subsequently popularized by the #MeToo hashtag in 2017), to ask her to help "do damage control."[1] Instead, she criticized the incident, prompting Robbins to later issue an apology: "I apologize for suggesting anything other than my profound admiration for the #MeToo movement."[2]

Although his late apology was a step in the right direction, its lack of specificity and sincerity read as inauthentic; as a result, many were hesitant to accept it. Although some applaud Robbins' teachings, which are rooted in personal empowerment and not victimhood, his comments laid bare his lack of knowledge of, and compassion for, what had grown to be a massive, important, and cathartic conversation for survivors of sexual abuse and trauma.

Knowledge and compassion are critical when we start to consider how we might move through the different stages of the Inclusive Leader Continuum—and that is never truer than at the Unaware stage.

Finding Your Way into the Conversation

If you are not someone who has been directly affected by adversity due to your identity, inclusion may not be one of your top priorities. There's a good chance you haven't noticed all the ways you can become more involved in supporting inclusion at work. Or maybe you're wondering what you can possibly contribute, or if it's your place to get involved at all. This chapter will help open your mind to what you've been overlooking or misinterpreting.

A key part of this stage is understanding **intent versus impact**. As you try to become more aware, you might find yourself focusing on your good intentions. They might make you feel better about who you are and reinforce the image you have of yourself as a good person. But unless those good thoughts make it out of your head and into supportive actions, you aren't actually helping anyone. This might sound obvious on paper, but many leaders are unaware that they need to bridge the gap between intent and impact to create real progress. For example, expressing good intent sometimes sounds like this: "Oh, I have daughters, so I understand the struggles women face." No doubt this is true, but wishing that gender discrimination would end is not the same as reporting harassment you've witnessed in the workplace or speaking up when locker room talk enters the board room—two actions that can actually help change the status quo.

It's important to note that, on some level, having personal connections to those who do not have the same access to opportunities as we do does actually build our empathy. A single conversation about divisive issues or a person's painful experience of exclusion can make us aware of the struggles we haven't experienced firsthand, and it can change our minds about stereotypes. These interactions can be key in helping us move beyond intentions. However, we ultimately want to reach a point where we don't need firsthand accounts from excluded individuals to notice and empathize with their struggles.

Humility

Catalyst, a leading think tank focused on diversity and inclusion, conducted a global study in 2014 where they sought to determine perceptions of inclusive leadership across six countries. The study revealed that one of the most significant indicators of an inclusive leader is *humility,* which they defined as "admitting mistakes, learning from criticism and different points of view, acknowledging and seeking contributions of others to overcome one's limitations."[3] In this context, the measure of your leadership is not having a perfect performance, but acknowledging an imperfect performance. This is important to realize because, when you commit to personal development, you have to admit that your past behaviors and actions were not always perfect.

Wade Davis, former NFL football player and motivational speaker, says that the compulsive need to be right is a big obstacle to building inclusion, particularly for the men he works with. That's why he begins every training with this question: "Can you agree for today to be uninterested in being right?" In agreeing to his request, participants feel the relief of not having to know everything. Instead, they get to be present and stay open to what they don't know. Wade's second question—"For today, can you be uninterested in thinking of yourself as a good person?"—is another key way to help people focus on humility and growth.[4]

Having all the right answers isn't important (and is not possible, anyway). Wanting to learn and grow through vulnerability is the name of the game. Inclusive leaders are aware of a bias toward rapid, decisive action and displays of power in the workplace, but they intentionally choose the inclusive response for each situation, even when it means slowing down the proverbial train to ask questions, to investigate, and to take care of a situation that needs to be remedied.

In 2010, the *New York Times* named **mansplaining** as one of the "Words of the Year."[5] The word originates from men underestimating how much the person they are talking to—often a woman—understands because they believe themselves (men) to be more knowledgeable. Basically, the man needlessly explains something the listener likely knows just as much about, if not more. Consultant and author Kim Goodwin was asked (unprompted) by two male colleagues how they could tell if they were mansplaining. She created a flowchart (see Figure 2.1[6]) to help them understand whether their explanation would likely come across as helpful or condescending.

I don't want to single out men here, however. *Splaining* can happen whenever a conversation occurs between two people in which one person holds, relatively speaking, more power or privilege and assumes they have the intellectual upper hand. Hence whitesplaining, straight-splaining, able(-bodied)splaining, wealthysplaining, thinsplaining, and so on. Those who splain may have the intent of helping the situation, but the actual impact of their actions can feel condescending or insulting. This communication problem stems from the splainer lacking many things—like good listening skills and patience—but it comes back to humility.

Ellen Leanse, author of *The Happiness Hack*, uses a phrase from her favorite teacher, Pamela Weiss, a Buddhist scholar: "When you feel a sense of judgment, ask yourself, 'What do I not yet understand?'"[7] Focus your attention on understanding, rather than submitting to the primal urge in your brain to protect yourself at any

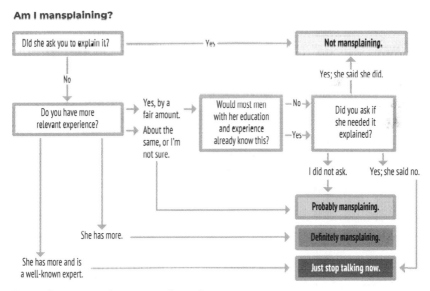

Figure 2.1. Mansplaining Explained

cost. If you can redirect your intention toward learning rather than getting defensive, the experience will have a more positive impact.

When you give up the need to be right and instead become curious about what you don't know—suspending judgment as you educate yourself about the reality of someone else's situation—you open yourself up to learn more about how you can ensure others feel welcomed, valued, respected, and heard. In the process, you adopt an attitude of humility. You make more informed decisions and avoid making costly mistakes or causing unnecessary harm to the people around you.

> *When you give up the need to be right and instead become curious, you open yourself up to learn how you can ensure others feel welcomed, valued, respected, and heard.*

Identifying Common Deflections

Let's dig deeper into our internal language that keeps us in the Unaware stage of the continuum. First, it's important to realize that any kind of change takes work. It's almost always easier to keep doing whatever we've been doing than try to do something differently. But change is baked into the process of becoming an inclusive leader. It starts with accountability. I connected with Chuck Shelton, CEO of Greatheart Consulting, to compile the following **deflections,** which are statements or beliefs that make an attempt to avoid accountability.[8] The following statements express viewpoints that might work in the moment, but ultimately keep you stuck in the status quo and prevent you from becoming a more inclusive leader.

- "I'm buried. I don't have time to prioritize this work."
- "I don't think we have any major issues here."
- "I don't feel comfortable discussing this."
- "I prefer to see past [race/gender/etc.]; we're all just people."
- "This is the way we've always done things."
- "It's not my fault I can't pronounce their name" (and/or forget someone's desired pronoun).
- "I didn't mean to offend anyone."
- "I'm fair minded."
- "She's a woman, so that's probably why she was hired."
- "We have a Head of Diversity and Inclusion so we are already dedicated to making changes."
- "We had mandatory unconscious bias training for all our employees, so we have already addressed this issue."

It may be very uncomfortable to uncover your reasoning for expressing these go-to reactions, but the sooner you can shift your thinking away from them, the better. Start by asking the following questions, honestly and openly:

- Am I relying or dependent on old behaviors? Why? In what ways do they continue to serve me? In what ways do they not?
- What's getting in the way of my ability to be inclusive?
- Am I proactively focused on trying to be more open (less skeptical) and more willing to accept (rather than deflect)?
- Am I harboring biases that affect my actions?

Understanding Bias

When you haven't supported inclusion in the workplace as well as you could have, the root cause is often *bias,* which can be unconscious. Bias reduces our ability to make decisions based on fairness, merit, and objectivity. These biases are rooted in our *primal brain,* a primitive biological holdover from a time when our ancestors needed to fight or take flight from saber-toothed tigers. But modern human brains have a *neocortex* that gives us the ability to intellectually transcend primal urges, allowing us to self-correct for biases and to make choices based on preference or will.

Don't get me wrong—overcoming biases can still be tough. As we live and move in this complex world, we shortcut a massive amount of data in order to make quick decisions. Viewed in its most positive aspect, bias is a way for our brains to simplify many streams of complex stimuli in a way to maximize our efficiency. The problem is that our brains often make the wrong assumptions.

The bias I see people struggle with most often is **confirmation bias**—the tendency to seek or notice information that confirms a belief and to avoid or ignore information that contradicts it. We are essentially hardwired to think we're right about things, rather than consider whether we're wrong. Since this happens at the subconscious level, it's hard to catch yourself in the act and realize when you're experiencing a confirmation bias.

As a consultant, I have witnessed such situations many times. For example, some male leaders believe that women don't work as hard as men or put in the same hours as men because they have more family-related needs that interfere with their performance. When a leader who holds this belief notices a gender wage gap with his employees, he might think the gap is justified because he believes women aren't as dedicated to their jobs. Instead of considering other causes of the gender wage gap, he uses the data to reconfirm his bias that women don't work as hard and therefore deserve less.

When you have these kinds of biases, you can unknowingly misread all kinds of situations, which is especially problematic when you have team members who are counting on you. For example, this same leader sees in his report that Jim makes more than Sally, but he also notices that Sally talks more about the time she spends with family. Jim may spend the same amount of time with family, but since he doesn't talk about it, the leader assumes he is more focused on work than Sally. The pay gap then becomes a positive proof point contributing to the leader's continued belief that women don't work as hard, and that's why they don't make as much. We all have confirmation biases, and you can see how they can be harmful in the workplace. Good leaders become aware of their biases, work to see fresh perspectives, and consult objective data.

Bias doesn't just affect the way we see others—it affects the way we view ourselves and our aptitude in supporting diversity and inclusion. For example, **self-enhancement bias** is the unconscious tendency to boost your self-esteem and overestimate your abilities, especially in situations of threat or failure.[9] A classic 1977 study showed that over 90 percent of professors rated themselves as better than average at teaching; two-thirds believed they were within the top 25 percent.[10] (Clearly this math did not add up.) Although these kinds of beliefs can be great for self esteem, they can also be harmful because they prevent us from acknowledging the truth about our capabilities. With inclusion, when we think we're doing a better job than we actually are, we are less likely to take further action, thus preventing real progress.

McKinsey and Company's Alexis Krivkovich shared with me that only 51 percent of managers say they know what to do to help improve gender diversity. "When only half of your workforce at the pivotal role of leadership deep in the organization knows what to do, the thought that you're going to see widespread change at a significant, accelerated pace is very unlikely."[11] And when you factor in the self-enhancement bias, the number of leaders who are actually prepared to drive change is probably much lower than half.

Krivkovich also shared that there are other knowledge and awareness gaps related to bias that thwart action. Very often, people have what we call **unconscious bias,** meaning they have little to no awareness of their biases. As such, they don't notice when the work environment supports those biases. When McKinsey administered a survey that asked "Do your managers challenge biased language when they see it occur?" three quarters of respondents said no. Those leaders may not be actively ignoring biases in the workplace; it's possible that they just don't see them.

For example, I know a man who works at a software company that has some curious demographics. There are many Asian Americans, Indian Americans, and immigrants from European countries in the company, so in many ways, the company has a lot of diversity—except, out of 300 employees, not one is Black. Whatever is preventing the company from hiring this demographic indicates that unconscious bias is at work in its hiring process. Perhaps its leaders would have been delighted to hire non-white job candidates from the very beginning but never considered how the hiring process somehow left Black professionals out of the conversation— for example, perhaps it unconsciously overlooked candidates from historically black colleges and universities. Years later, the optics are hard to ignore, and the reality is exponentially more difficult to undo.

Krivkovich explained that we are, to a large degree, inheriting an unbalanced environment as a result of pattern build-up. That's why it's so important to keep our eyes open and notice when things don't look right. Making change often starts with an open dialogue—one that is not accusatory or emotionally charged but is focused on the constructive—one that asks "How do we build from here forward?"

The supposition isn't that you are malicious because you have biases; although some leaders cling to their biases (and those who do may need to read and reread this chapter several times...), many are uncomfortable and even ashamed when they're made aware of them. It is not a proud moment when you realize that not only are you biased, but that your workplace was built by only some people to work for only some people—and that many in the same workplace feel that it's an awkward fit, at best. Some feel that they are expected to contort themselves to be successful at work, constantly making painful choices between trying to fit in and being authentic. This is a difficult and unhealthy road to the future.

If you can give up the need to be right, prevent yourself from becoming offended, and ask, from a place of genuine curiosity, "Might this be something else?" you can take the opportunity to challenge the past and use your voice to shape a better future.

Uncovering Bias: Questions to Ask

An important process for this stage in the continuum is to dig into your biases to acknowledge them and better understand them. Spend some time reflecting on the following questions:

- Where am I exposed to difference? Where can I go to be in the company of people who are different from me?

- Am I intentional about placing myself in new communities and conversations? If so, which ones?

- In the past, have I assumed that I'm doing enough on the topic of inclusion?

- In which areas do I need to build my knowledge?

- Where is bias intruding on my ability to be an effective colleague, leader, or friend?

Overcoming Bias

Becoming aware of your biases is the first step toward solving them. The next step is exploring them to gain a deeper understanding of your feelings. Our brains naturally put things into categories based on our experiences, so if you have a particularly positive or negative experience with a certain demographic, that could create feelings of bias. This is especially true if you haven't had many (or any) other interactions with someone of a certain identity. When this happens, one of the best things you can do is to get to know the people who can help you break those stereotypes. When you get to know people on a personal level, it helps you see them as individuals rather than as just demographics.

Broaden Your Horizons

- Branch out and connect with more coworkers who look different from you. Make an effort to make small talk and be more social with people outside of your regular circle.

- Attend a meeting or event that exposes you to members of different communities.

- Ask questions that get other people to open up. This can be as simple as listening, and then responding with a question that invites the other person to expand. When you seem genuinely interested in other people's lives, they are more likely to let their walls down and show you their true selves. This moves coworker relationships beyond discussions of the weather and the tedious morning commute.

- Consume different media. Go for podcasts, TV shows, books, and movies where the people involved have different identities than you do.

Humbling yourself in this way can be intimidating, but it gets easier as you build your network, remain a constant presence, and become someone who can be trusted. Participation is a great first step and much appreciated. It does not go unnoticed.

Listening plays a big role in overcoming bias and becoming a more inclusive leader. Bernard T. Ferrari, McKinsey alumnus and dean of the Carey Business School at Johns Hopkins University, sums up the key steps to becoming a better listener: show respect, keep quiet, and challenge assumptions.[12] I have adapted these steps to reflect what it means to be an aware and inclusive leader:

SHOW RESPECT The most effective leader equally respects the opinion of every employee and recognizes that good ideas come from people with different experiences. They solicit those contributions and moderate discussions to ensure contributors are comfortable to share in the first place.

KEEP QUIET Inclusive leaders should know when to stay quiet and let others take the reins. Consider the 80/20 rule in which your conversation partner speaks 80 percent of the time and you speak the other 20 percent. Even then, be aware of when you can use your 20 percent to speak up in support of someone who may not be heard, and not just on your own behalf.

CHALLENGE ASSUMPTIONS The best listeners are always on the lookout for assumptions being made in a conversation, including their own. They will ask questions to gain clarity and not be afraid to let go of their own assumptions.

Even well-intentioned, seasoned leaders can benefit from this list as a reminder. To get direct reports, managers, and colleagues talking, author, speaker, and professional baseball player Mike Robbins offers a favorite question in his book, *Bring Your Whole Self to Work*: "Is there anything you need or any way I can support you right now?"[13] This question invites people to open up and shows that you're on their side.

Inside Circle Inventory

Inclusive leaders traveling the continuum must make a regular habit of examining their inner circle of contacts. When they do this for the first time, and even subsequent times, they often find that this circle reflects a positive bias for those who are most like them. We all have our go-to people. They may be coworkers, friends, those we mentor, as well as those who mentor us. It might be easiest to think of this list as those we talk to the most frequently, whether the setting is work or not.

The simple exercise of inventorying the diverse dimensions *different from ours* forces us to look for patterns in our relationships, our tendency to seek comfort in sameness, and our discomfort with the unknown.

Try writing down the names of your trusted inside circle in the first column of a grid such as the one provided in Table 1. Next, fill in the top row with various diversity dimensions, such as the examples I've provided in the bulleted list that follows the table. You can even total up the X marks to get a birds-eye view of where there is a lack of representation, of difference, in your daily life.

INITIALS OR FIRST NAME (NO FAMILY MEMBERS)*	DIVERSITY DIMENSIONS				
	ETHNICITY	AGE	GENDER	ETC.	TOTAL Xs
Person 1	X		X		2
Person 2		X			1
Person 3			X		1
Etc.					
Total Xs	1	1	2		

*Place an X only if descriptors are different than your own identity.

Table 1. Inner Circle Inventory

Just having this knowledge helps you understand whether you are mostly surrounded by people who are much like you. When that happens, it's easy to exist in a bubble that's devoid of diverse perspectives and experiences. As an inclusive leader, stepping outside of this bubble will help advance your journey on the continuum.

Here are a number of examples of diversity dimensions you might include:

- Ethnicity
- Age
- Gender
- Gender identity and expression
- Sexual orientation
- Education
- Abilities
- Marital status
- Parenting status
- Political beliefs
- Socioeconomic background

An Important Distinction

An important distinction to make at this stage is that inclusive leaders are less concerned with **equality** than with the concept of **equity**. *Equality* is something easy to support, because it's a far-off, idealized goal. *Equity,* on the other hand, implies that we understand that the playing field is uneven, since we don't all start from the same place and we don't have the same opportunities.

Michelle Obama talks a lot about equity in her book *Becoming*. When she hosted events at the White House, she made it a priority to invite children from minority and impoverished communities. Those children do not typically have the same level of access to quality education and enrichment activities as those from other communities, and she wanted to level the playing field by giving them valuable experiences they might not otherwise have had.

In the workplace, we can think about equity in much the same way to address the systemic blind spots that perpetuate unequal outcomes.[14] Maybe you didn't intend to build or support an unfair reality, but you can change it, now that you are learning how. This is every leader's most sacred responsibility, particularly if their road to leadership has been smoother because of their identity.

> *Maybe you didn't intend to build or support an unfair reality, but you can change it now that you are learning how.*

Another way to understand the difference between equality and equity is to realize that addressing equity issues strikes at the source of the problem rather than dealing with the symptoms, one by one. Our attachment to the **myth of meritocracy**—which is the notion that companies are structured to reward only the most talented and determined individuals[15]—is increasingly being viewed as out of touch because it doesn't acknowledge our very real differences, and how much harder the journey up the ladder, or even *onto* the ladder, is for some.

An insightful article by author Amy Sun makes this clear:

> *Treating everyone exactly the same actually is not fair. What equal treatment does do is erase our differences and promote privilege. Equity is giving everyone what they need to be successful. Equality is treating everyone the same.*[16]

Surrounding Yourself with a Trusted Few

If you've recognized some of yourself in this chapter, you're likely feeling motivated to take a closer look at your potential to be a more inclusive leader. Similarly, if you want to support your colleagues in their journey out of Unawareness, this chapter has likely provided many points of entry to transformational conversations.

It's important to note that this stage of your journey might be somewhat private. If you realize you haven't given certain people a fair chance, you might not want to broadcast that to your colleagues. (Not only would this be damaging to your reputation, it could also make other people feel bad.) But as you become aware of your biases, you'll start to understand how you can do things differently to better support others. It is a learning process, and it helps to have support from people you trust. When you're ready, seek out conversations with a trusted few who can help you find your balance, your vocabulary, and begin to identify new skills. You can and should look forward to building and deepening these supportive one-on-one relationships as you travel the continuum. Indeed, they are the all-important fuel that you need to not only stay on top of what others are experiencing but also to take action as appropriate.

At this stage, newly enlightened leaders sometimes want to discuss their revelations about people they previously stereotyped with individuals who belong to those groups. Although honesty and openness can be great, I don't recommend this approach. First, it sounds like a plotline from the TV show *The Office,* which is hallmarked by awkward and inappropriate behavior at work. In the show, general manager Michael Scott constantly **tokenizes** his employees (the gay one, the Black one, the Indian one) to the point where his job security is always on the line. His workplace blunders make us laugh at him in his ignorance, but many real-life leaders come dangerously close to following in those footsteps.

If you *do* approach people outside your trusted circle, remember not to burden "the obvious choice" with teaching you about diversity and inclusion. Before you ask others to make time to mentor or support you, make sure you've already invested time and energy on your own. This is especially critical, because many of those who could teach you about their identity are experiencing the intense headwinds of being "the only" at work. This type of **emotional labor** can feel exhausting to them, especially when they are already using a lot of energy to suppress how they feel or who they are at work.

Next Steps

What we know is that inclusive leaders know when to lead from the front and, especially, when it is better to lead from behind or alongside. They focus on how best to be of service to others, or in a given situation. They check their egos at the door.[17]

Some of us are seen and heard more readily than others. The work of an inclusive leader is to recognize that your own experience of humility may look very different from that of others as a result of your relative status or influence. This is the product of how some have been traditionally more valued, while others have had to work much harder to be valued in the same way.

Although this chapter might have been an uncomfortable read, it likely brought at least one insightful moment to the surface for you about your own behaviors, or perhaps it equipped you to better understand the beliefs or assumptions of others that prevent them from stepping into the Inclusive Leader Continuum. As we prepare to transition to Aware, consider the research and data you might not have been aware of before you read this chapter, the ways that our language might need to be reevaluated, and what you are most curious to learn about next in your journey as an inclusive leader.

AS YOU WRAP UP THIS CHAPTER, TAKE A MOMENT TO REFLECT ON THE FOLLOWING QUESTIONS:

- What have I realized I know little about, or have only a cursory understanding of, when it comes to diversity-related experiences of others?

- Am I aware of bias when I see it, or do I (perhaps unwittingly) participate in it?

- Do I experience any resistance to learning more or having my beliefs challenged?

- Where could I begin to extend my intentions into greater awareness?

CHAPTER THREE

Aware

Empathy begins with understanding life from another person's perspective. Nobody has an objective experience of reality. It's all through our individual prisms.

—STERLING K. BROWN

Daniel was part of a vibrant African-American community in Atlanta, which meant that moving to a less-diverse and less multicultural state was a big culture shock for him. As Daniel tells it, on his first day at his new job, his new supervisor noticed him looking around for other people who looked like him and not seeing anyone who did. At the end of that first day the supervisor assured Daniel that, even though he wasn't African-American and didn't know everything Daniel would need as an African-American, he would do everything he could to give Daniel everything he'd need. Instead of pretending Daniel would have the same cultural experience in the company as other employees who shared an identity, the supervisor had the courage to address the elephant in the room upfront. Although he may have risked making Daniel feel singled out, the supervisor approached the situation with tact, compassion, and an eagerness to help. He went on to do everything in his power to help Daniel grow into the leader he is today—he showed him the ropes at the company, he was always in Daniel's corner, and he became one of Daniel's earliest mentors.

That experience had a pass-it-forward effect. Now Daniel looks for ways in which he can mentor people who don't look like him in addition to supporting other African-American employees. He wants to help people dream bigger and make a world of difference for them, just like his mentor did for him.

This success story is built around awareness. Daniel's mentor was paying attention, listening (perhaps especially for what was unspoken), and offering support without assuming what that support might look like.

Shifting Your Perspective

The next step in the Inclusive Leader Continuum is learning to listen with an open and curious mind to different communities of people—especially those who you are perhaps less familiar with—and to be truly present to receiving information that's new or challenging to you so that you can grow in awareness.

Awareness is a powerful stage in the inclusive leader's journey. You could argue that this stage is one that no one ever leaves because you continue cycling back to it, sometimes painfully, as you learn about different people and communities. For the inclusive leader, this stage should be like a home base. You will always be absorbing new knowledge around different identities—or diversity dimensions—and as the culture continually changes, it is worth it to constantly revisit shifts in language. As you deepen your own self-knowledge, you are again destined to return.

Humility is still key to this stage of your journey. Anytime you believe you know everything about one community, the Aware mindset reminds you that that is not possible. Even if you are a member of that particular community, it's possible that you still have more truth you need to uncover in terms of how others have been affected, or how you yourself have been affected by exclusion and inequality. It is challenging to decide to live from a new mindset, and awkward to be reminded of how fallible you are, but it is a challenge that you must accept.

Perhaps you relish learning; like a sponge, you're hungry for more understanding as you imagine the experiences of others, and you're fueled by curiosity about the human experience in all of its variations. As you learn, some unpleasant facts emerge that demand to be more broadly understood; for instance, 61 percent of employees feel they need to cover key parts of who they are because they fear negative stereotypes, and nearly 50 percent of LGBTQ+ employees remain closeted in the workplace.[1]

As you shift your perspective, you may notice that you have been unengaged, inactive, and harmful to others. In your inattention, or in your resistance, you may have missed that you have many tools you can use to make yourself a better leader and improve the feeling of belonging in others.

As you grow in awareness, you may learn more about how your experiences have shaped your identity, which will help you discover your unique voice to champion change. You may have experienced your differences as negatives until now, and you may continue to choose not to disclose certain personal stories, but the good news is that this stage can be about reawakening; you can use those differences as fuel as you become re-inspired about what you *can* do. Perhaps you can even leave frustrating experiences behind in order to take a fresh, more optimistic look at what is within your sphere of control.

The knowledge you accumulate at this stage can challenge some deeply held ideas you have about fairness, hard work, and how advantages and disadvantages have informed your life. Everyone has been shaped through circumstances outside their control, from primary dimensions—like age, ethnicity, and ability—to secondary dimensions—such as family, religion, and socioeconomic background. You can't change any of these, of course; they were either inborn or inherited and have been carried forward by you as circumstances of your lived experience. You have built awareness about your own diversity dimensions by noticing others' reactions to you, whether they are positive/negative, fair/unfair, and so on. This stage of the continuum is about becoming aware of other people's experiences in this regard and understanding the gaps that can be bridged to cultivate an environment where others feel more welcomed, valued, respected, and heard.

Throughout this book, my hope is that you'll find yourself becoming sensitized to the concept that you may have struggled in some ways and not in others, and that, as a result, you have some raw materials, which you probably aren't using yet, that you can leverage to build trusted relationships with others. Before the Aware stage, you likely haven't thought of yourself as having these assets, but it is an exciting discovery that can unify you with others, through all your dimensions, shared and otherwise.

> *"When people are faced with open and non-judgmental listening, they are able to say who they really are in the world. They're able to express themselves fully, and what that brings is freedom."*
>
> —PAUL BROWDE[2]

Understanding Privilege

As you become aware, it's important to educate yourself about your claim—or lack thereof—to special advantages not freely available to everyone else. *Privilege* is something that is afforded to certain people by society and in the workplace, often offering them invisible benefits that people of another status cannot access. It can be defined as the extent to which one has access to something that another does not. Privileges can relate to race, class, gender, sexual orientation, language, geographical location, ability, and religion, to name a few.[3]

Privilege can also include someone's socioeconomic status.[4] For example, if you can buy what you need and want without worry, are not seen as a threat in higher socioeconomic communities, and are more likely to be believed innocent by the criminal justice system, you have access to class privilege.

Some pushback surrounds the concept of privilege, as if admitting our privileges somehow invalidates how hard we have worked to achieve certain advantages not available to others. We may assume that the label *privilege* implies we don't deserve to have what we have or infers that we have never experienced hardship. But privilege on its own isn't bad. Talking about it is not an invalidation but rather an acknowledgment that those individuals who are not straight, able bodied or white, for example, are likely to have worked even harder to achieve what they have in a world where the aforementioned identities are valued relatively more.

When the role of privilege isn't understood by leaders who've unwittingly benefited from it, I find they are less understanding of the particular difficulties some face in their organizations. I've included here two team exercises that can be used to illustrate how different identities relate to privilege—for better or worse.

The first exercise is called the **privilege walk**.[5] It offers a way to uncover some of the advantages and disadvantages people experienced growing up, and perhaps continue to experience now, so they can lead from a more self-aware place. Participants stand in a horizontal line, and the facilitator reads a series of statements. These statements address privilege stemming from race, gender and gender identity, class, sexual orientation, ability, and more. Throughout the exercise, individuals move forward or backward as they respond to the following statements. (Although this is ultimately meant to be a team exercise, as you're reading this, I recommend reflecting privately on the topics.)

- If you were born in the United States, take one step forward.

- If your ancestors came to the United States by force, take one step back.

- If you went to college, take one step forward.

- If you took out loans for your education, take one step back.

- If you have ever been the only person of your race/gender/ socioeconomic status/sexual orientation in a classroom or workplace setting, please take one step back.

- If you have ever been diagnosed as having a physical or mental illness/disability, take one step back.

- If you would never think twice about calling the police when trouble occurs, take one step forward.

- If you can show affection for your romantic partner in public without fear of ridicule or violence, take one step forward.

- If you get time off for your religious holidays, take one step forward.

- If you feel comfortable walking home alone at night, take one step forward.

- If you have ever felt like there was *not* adequate or accurate representation of your racial group, sexual orientation group, gender group, and/or disability group in the media, take one step back.

During this exercise, many participants are afraid to look around the room, while others feel shame about being in the front or at the back. This simple, yet powerful, exercise allows participants to check the assumptions they make about those around them. Suddenly, participants can clearly see the unique combination of advantages and disadvantages they each face.

Although this exercise is great for raising awareness of our different experiences, it does have a few critical drawbacks to watch out for.[6] For starters, the privilege walk depends on people with underprivileged identities disclosing their experiences in order to make a point for those with more privilege. Though this can be a powerful experience, it puts participants with less privilege in the tricky situation of bearing the weight of the exercise and can create feelings of shame for all participants along the privilege spectrum. Therefore, facilitating this exercise requires careful navigation to acknowledge and then transition those feelings of shame into a call to action. As an alternative, participants can answer each of the questions privately and tally up their score before sharing with the group. That way, everyone in the room can do the exercise without having to reveal anything that may feel compromising.

Another exercise known as "Privilege for Sale" is growing in popularity and provides an additional alternative.[7] In this activity, participants are split into groups and asked to pick which privileges they would choose to buy from a provided list, each with varying prices. Each group, however, is given a different amount of "money" to use, highlighting the fact that not everyone in life has the same access to these privileges. This activity is more collaborative and less individual-focused, which can help unify the participants instead of isolating them in shameful emotions.

Both exercises have their unique advantages and specific purposes, and you may find one to be more effective than the other depending on the situation. The purpose is not to make people who are more or less privileged feel bad or to call out differences between colleagues. The purpose is to build awareness that some people have a heavier load to carry on their path to success. That understanding is crucial if you are to move forward along the continuum.

Stories of Origin: Time to Dig In

As you learn how little you know—about yourself, and others—you may find the need to do some serious self-reflection. You likely have a story in which you have personally experienced adversity, exclusion, felt your difference, or perhaps been up close and personal with a loved one who has had to wrestle with being more or less accepted. You have a *story of origin,* because you've lived through a new realization, an aha moment, a lesson learned, or a profound life experience, and often those moments are ones of discomfort, uncertainty, and loss.

I mentioned earlier that I was drawn toward diversity and inclusion work when I was in my twenties. But what I didn't mention was that this passion came about only after my childhood dream fell through. I was raised in a musical family and always wanted to pursue a performing career. I loved singing and I was good at it. Really good. I was ecstatic when I moved to New York City to become an opera singer and follow my dreams.

It wasn't long before my personal identity was wrapped into operatic singing. It was who I was and what I loved. I felt lucky to be so sure of my talents and my place in this world. But just when my life's path seemed so clear, things started to go wrong. In the course of my training, I injured my voice and needed vocal surgery. Like many surgeries, the recovery was long and painful, and I required a lot of rest to heal. There were weeks when I wasn't able to speak at all—not even a whisper. And when I finally felt like I was doing better, my voice would get injured again and I'd need another surgery.

Throughout this time, I was going through a mental and emotional crisis as well as a physical one. What a lot of people don't realize is that there's a huge stigma in the industry about vocal surgery. Who would want to hire me if I wasn't reliable? Just like a professional athlete downplays injuries, I tried to make people believe I was healthy and that everything was normal. I was like a swan who appeared to be gracefully gliding above the water, but who was paddling hard under the surface just to keep up. More than anything, I felt so much shame. The world of performance that had long been part of my core identity suddenly made me feel like an outsider. I had to work through some heartbreaking implications for my career and start to explore who I was outside that world. In the end, my instrument was forever compromised, so I had to tap into a larger sense of purpose and find a new direction in my life.

Although this was one of the most painful things I've ever been through, it led me to my current career trajectory, which has been immensely rewarding. When I interpret the meaning of what happened to me, I like to say, "I was meant to use my voice, just not as a singer." I've shared my story with audiences all over the world, and I was initially shocked by how many people can relate to it. So many people have come up to me after events to tell me about how something similar happened to them, but in a totally different way. These experiences of fighting through adversity make us who we are, and we come out stronger. This strength alone is inspirational to others, encouraging them to keep going.

The experiences that form your stories of origin will reveal themselves over time, but if you don't invite them to the fore and consider how you might use them, you aren't living up to your potential as an inclusive leader. The passage of time, with its healing powers and its ability to enable you to see your experiences from a safe distance as the teachers that they are, is a gift. This wisdom doesn't just appear; it needs to be worked at, pulled out, and examined. It can gain meaning and significance through being articulated, first to yourself, and then in a safe space with others.

As you invite new perspectives like this, it can be a fragile time, one in which you need to be careful of judging yourself and others. You might fall into the trap of feeling badly about yourself, thinking, "What could I possibly share about myself that might be helpful to others?" But when you give yourself permission to dive deeper into some of the universal human experiences that we all share (but don't typically talk about), you'll begin to understand the parts of your life that can help you better relate to other people. It's critical that you don't kill storytelling before it begins or apply value judgments.

To help you go beyond the statements in the privilege walk exercise, take a look at the following questions. These may help you in the excavation process and can be navigated as part of a team exercise, with the help of a friend or mentor, or even solo, as writing prompts:

- What was your life like growing up? Did you experience any hardship not shared by some or all of your peers?

- When have you felt the sting of exclusion in your life? What did that feel like? How did you navigate that?

- Can you share a story that reveals a bias you've overcome or helped someone else to overcome?

- Describe an encounter you've had with someone different from you (e.g., from a different race, class, gender, sexual orientation, language, geographical location, ability, or religion) that influenced you in a positive way.

- Alternatively, describe an encounter you've had with someone different from you that influenced you in a *negative* way, and consider why. Was it uncomfortable because of assumptions or biases that affected the experience in the wrong way? How could the experience have been valuable or positive if you had thought or acted differently?

- Describe an encounter you've had with someone different from you that made a difference to *them* in a positive way.

At this stage, simply having a grasp of all the threads that make up your story is enough. In the next chapter, I'll start to discuss how you might find ways to share your story with others to further inclusion and to ensure others feel less alone. Perhaps you'll be able to inspire others to work on and share their own stories one day.

Some leaders have a lot of personal experiences to consider when they think about inclusion. This would certainly describe Kathy Martinez, leader of the People with Disabilities Segment at Wells Fargo. She shares that she progressed out of the closet over several years in a series of roles, from the Bush Administration, to the World Institute on Disability, to being a role model as a blind Latina lesbian professional leading an entire bank's strategy for the disabilities community.

Anyone who knows Martinez knows she leads with a big heart and lots of humor. She jokingly refers to herself as a "triple minority" and laughs in recalling her mother's response to her coming out, "'Oh, my God, why are you choosing this? You're blind, you're Latina, you're a woman. Why would you pick this too?' She thought I was trying to compete in the Oppression Olympics or something!"[8]

When I spoke with Wade Davis, he shared how vulnerable he felt as a young, gay football player in the hyper-masculine world of sports and thus remained closeted. He was living his dream and his nightmare at the same time. "You learned these notions [of shame] as a little boy, and you take them on into these other spaces."[9] Today, Davis is not only an out LGBTQ+ advisor to the NFL—a position where he can directly impact the coaches, owners, and players by sharing what would have made the NFL a more welcoming space for someone like him—but he also now identifies most strongly as a feminist. He is especially dedicated to getting men to start redefining ideas of masculinity.

When you can dig into your past experiences and better understand how they shaped your life, you'll be in a better position to help others through similar challenges. As you uncover how your identities have been shaped by privilege—or a lack thereof—you not only discover your origin stories, but also in what areas and instances your life has been easier or, indeed, harder than for others. You begin to understand just how unequal the playing field really is. Your eyes begin to open to the obstacles you have come up against, as well as those others have had to overcome. Armed with your newfound knowledge, you may feel embarrassed or even angry on behalf of yourself or someone else. You may want to speak up on behalf of a certain group or individual, but feel afraid to do so, for fear of saying the wrong thing. You may even feel overwhelmed or paralyzed by the sheer weight of the truths you uncover—like, for example, the experiences of Nicole Sanchez, a well-respected diversity consultant. In a long Twitter thread, she described the gulf between our experiences and how they shape our ability to show up fully at work. (As an aside, note that her comments include the word **Latinx,** pronounced "La-TEEN-ex." Latinx denotes Latin American origin or descent, and is a gender-neutral alternative to the standard *Latino* or *Latina*.)

> *In the past few years, I've been in the position to lead inside companies while major events, all with racism at their core, have unfolded in the news. From the unrelenting videos of police violence against our Black neighbors, to the presence of actual Nazis in our midst, to the Muslim travel ban, to the images of Latinx children in detention camps, leading "business as usual" is not an option.*
>
> *The reality inside most companies is that the people in the lead are not the ones most deeply affected. I cannot explain the feeling of walking into an office in the midst of these events and being asked with a smile "How*

was your weekend?" The answer is, "My weekend was a racist hellscape, thanks." And the extra painful part is being around people who have the luxury of not paying attention, not fearing for their family's safety, wondering why all the long faces.[10]

This is an example of how the narrowness of what's permitted at work harms so many, and how entrenched it is not to "see" others, even if you don't share experiences directly. The choice that Sanchez is forced to make, between authenticity and bringing her whole self to work, or choosing to rise above if she can and return to "business as usual," feels deeply unfair.

> *Employees wrestle with all sorts of things that are never discussed but that steer their lives, their engagement, and their productivity.*

Employees are wrestling with all sorts of things that are never discussed but that are steering their lives, their engagement, and their productivity. News of a transgender-troops ban in the military, or a shooting like the one that happened at the Pulse nightclub in Orlando, Florida, will spread like wildfire among anyone who identifies as LGBTQ+ or is an **ally** of the LGBTQ+ community; for example, parents of children who are questioning their gender identity or who are worried about whether their children will be safe in the world or have the same level of opportunity as others will also pay keen attention to such stories. Given what social neuroscientists call **distance biases,** however, you may not feel the impact if you aren't personally affected in some way and, therefore, you may devalue the significance of such events.[11] It's also difficult when we hear so many discriminatory stories in the news. It can be hard not to emotionally disconnect from it all, but doing so is not helpful for driving change. If your compassion or anger isn't activated when you hear of such things in the headlines, try thinking about how you would feel if your story of origin were strongly tied to the community experiencing hardship. This will help you gain the awareness of how personal these events can feel to people.

Even if you still feel like you're on the outside of these issues or believe certain problems don't pertain to you, you are still being impacted. Remember that our individual and collective productivity at work is bound up with each other's. Organizations are made up of working relationships in which we depend on each other to accomplish our work, to innovate, and to generate the next big idea. Every day, colleagues may be managing devastating news and messages that deeply affect their personal stories. If you've never experienced what this feels like and then been asked to shine at work, then you are extremely fortunate. Simply being aware that other people are going through such difficulties is a huge step toward becoming a more inclusive leader.

Intersectional Allyship

The concept of **intersectionality** was originated by Kimberlé Crenshaw.[12] She talked about it as being the nexus of multiple stigmatized identities. If you are a woman of color, for example, you have dual stigmatized identities. If you're a queer woman of color, you have triple intersecting stigmatized identities. If you're a queer woman of color with a plus-size body type, you have quadruple stigmatized identities. Each one of those identities carries its own implications in terms of a person's practical ability to be openly authentic and to be treated equitably.

You may discover that you have experienced both disadvantages *and* advantages because of your different intersecting identities. You can leverage the more privileged aspects of your identity to better support other marginalized groups who don't have access to the same opportunities as you. The Aware stage is all about unearthing the unseen advantages you already possess and considering how you can and should use them in service of inclusion.

Let me explain this concept by delving deeper into the LGBTQ+ community, which is actually a diverse collection of groups that share a history but contain a wide variety of every kind of diversity (and some specific challenges when it comes to inclusiveness). To illustrate, let's consider the example of a gay white man. Although this man is gay, he has many opportunities of access, comfort, and safety when compared to others in the same community who are, say, gender nonconforming or people of color. For this reason, he can use his male privilege to influence another man's behavior in a positive direction, or he can use the access he has to a male-dominated workplace to gain career exposure and visibility for a female colleague of color.

Creative and social entrepreneur Philip Patston is a gay white man with a disability who was inspired to enter the field of diversity and inclusion. Depending on the context, he recognized that he was both oppressed and oppressor:

> I realized that, predominantly, political labels are used to discount voices. In groups of white, non-disabled straight men, I was just the "gay disabled guy," but in groups of disabled, lesbian feminists of color, I was the oppressive "white guy." So I was inspired to create a new discourse around diversity, based on a new definition of diversity being the synergy of our uniqueness and commonality. This creates a more inquisitive response to diversity, rather than a fear or disdain of difference or an assumption that we're all the same.[13]

Tiffany Dufu, author of *Drop the Ball,* recently spoke to the responsibility she feels to use her privilege for others, as a woman of color:

> *My own responsibility involves being hyperaware of all the identities that have afforded me an advantage in our society. For example, I have benefited from being middle class, straight, able-bodied, and a size two.*[14]

"Thin privilege," or the social advantages granted to people based on body size,[15] functions similarly to other systems of privilege in that it grants certain individuals access to certain areas because of unearned or inherent characteristics.

Dufu points to an article by Reshma Saujani, the founder and CEO of Girls Who Code, as a reminder to be aware of different kinds of privilege. In the article, Saujani writes about a series of miscarriages she's had over the years. As she says, "It took me years to start talking publicly about my fertility struggles because, being bound up as so many women are in the perfection trap for so long, I was concerned about what those failed pregnancies said about me."[16] The pressure she felt was one Dufu hadn't experienced as a fertile woman, and Saujani's bravery in speaking out allowed Dufu to recognize another form of privilege.

Using myself as an example, I have two stigmatized identities, as an LGBTQ+ person and as a woman, but I also have my relatively privileged identity as a white person, with a socioeconomic background and a family stability that has meant more comfort and ease. These identities intersect in relevant ways. My ethnicity reflects the majority of senior leadership at most companies, for example, so my goal is to be an advocate for colleagues of color who may not be granted a similar level of access, or who struggle to be heard fully when they are. On the flip side, as a woman and as an LGBTQ+ person, I may, on some level, also benefit from male and straight allies helping me get into rooms that I can't get into on my own, to help bolster me, protect me, and use their influence and access on my behalf.

Every single one of us can be an effective ally to some community, regardless of the various intersections of our identities. And, in fact, the experience of intersectional impact is a great teacher, as we endeavor to grow and empathize. If you have any kind of privilege or access, you can use it on behalf of someone who doesn't.

Interrupting Bias

As adults, and as aspiring inclusive leaders, we have the great opportunity to challenge not just our wiring, but how we were raised, what we observed in our lifetimes that shaped our beliefs, and what responsibility we have now to those around us. But we need to be aware that we were raised with the biases of our parents and our communities, and that they became woven into our psyches. As cognitive neuroscience researchers like to say, if you have a brain, you're biased. It's universal neurobiology, and nothing personal. (For instance, you may notice that you only ever sit next to people who look like you in your workplace cafeteria, or you only ever recommend somebody for an opportunity if they have a similar educational background as you.) Once you understand that we all are biased, you have the cognitive ability to self-correct, and being biased becomes a choice. This new awareness, and then the ability to choose different behavior or action, is the measure of our character as inclusive leaders.

Some of these biases may have become more deeply rooted if you haven't seen diverse examples of professionals in a variety of fields. Take, for example, the media. The lack of diversity in the media you consume may be contributing to your biases by implicitly telling you who belongs where and how they're supposed to function in that profession. But the good news is that more and more people are noticing who's missing from the popular culture landscape. We are collecting the data, and the disparities are beginning to generate some attention.

And, if you thought the media was lagging behind on diversity, corporate America is even worse. In 2017, only sixteen of the Fortune 500 companies shared detailed employee demographic information (very telling, in and of itself). Within senior management and executives of those companies (5,089 people), 80 percent are men, and 72 percent are white men.[17] The Equal Employment Opportunity Commission reports that from 1985 to 2014, Black men in management rose from 3 percent to 3.3 percent.[18] Meanwhile, Black women still only constitute 1.5 percent of senior management in the Fortune 500. Considering that white men make up only 42 percent of the labor force, these stats are clearly problematic.[19] When you see very little diversity at the top levels of all kinds of companies, it's hard not to get a picture in your head about who belongs there and who doesn't. In this way, the problem is self-perpetuating.

At this point in the continuum, the goal is not to eliminate bias, which is in fact neurobiologically impossible, but to generate awareness. You *can* learn to correct for bias. You can create new pathways to question business as usual.

A great way to continue working past our biases is to participate in unconscious bias training. These programs create aha moments for people who are unaware of an issue that is leading to inequities in the workplace. It is a popular approach because, when you look at your biases, it can be truly shocking, and shock and surprise can lead to a shift, a new insight, and new behaviors. It may also lead to feelings of guilt and shame, but these feelings shouldn't hamper your journey or put it on hold indefinitely.

It's in your power to recognize when your biases and your behaviors are not serving you. And sometimes, it's not you—but that doesn't mean you're off the hook. By not challenging bias when you see it in others, you're enabling a biased system to continue to cause harm.

Disrupting Bias in the Media

A common blind spot in journalism is the lack of women and people of color quoted in reporting. This can be attributed to a multitude of factors, such as a biased perception of which voices are credible, or an overreliance on established networks that fail to include diverse perspectives. *Bloomberg* reporter Ben Bartenstein noticed this tendency in his own reporting, saying, "[In 2017], just 13% of sources I quoted (62 in total) were women. I was appalled. Here I was thinking and talking about diversity on a daily basis, yet my own work didn't hold up to snuff."[20]

Following this realization, Bartenstein made a commitment to include a wider variety of sources in 2018. He and his colleagues began curating a roster of prominent women on their beat from which they could pull quotes, and by the end of the year, half of the sources Bartenstein quoted were women. Just by making an effort to look for more diverse voices, Bartenstein's team discovered an untapped pool of talent that gave them an edge over their competitors.

Still, Bartenstein warns against tokenizing diverse voices purely for the sake of appearing inclusive: "We didn't quote them because they were women. We quoted them because they were the most qualified to answer our questions on a given topic, yet somehow got overlooked in the past." Indeed, diverse sourcing goes beyond meeting a quota. Diverse sourcing leads to more interesting and reputable reporting, and eventually, should become so ingrained in the process that it becomes second nature.

No Quick Fix

As you listen and become more aware of the real issues so many are facing in your workplace and beyond, you may begin wondering why diversity and inclusion continue to be a persistent issue in workplaces and why things haven't improved. Perhaps you're even questioning why you never knew the things you're learning about through actively listening to other people's stories—or, if you knew them, why taking some kind of action wasn't a priority for you before. You may begin to reconsider a lot of things.

Part of the problem for leaders is that, in the organizational world, they like to "solve" things, and quickly. You may be paid to problem-solve every day, so it's not a surprise that you would try to apply this lens to what is a complex and multifaceted, multilayered reality that needs greater care and a more nuanced approach. Inequities in our society and in our workplaces have been built, enabled, and perpetuated over many years. Power tends to protect power. Challenging the status quo is, at the least, inconvenient and, at the most, downright threatening to others.

Power tends to protect power. Challenging the status quo is, at the least, inconvenient and, at the most, downright threatening to others.

Anand Giridharadas, author of the bestselling book *Winners Take All*, shares that in business, we tend to look at problems like we look at fixing an engine (clear solutions, quickly executed, and then on to the next), instead of problems, which are more like crime scenes:

Problems with an engine need to be tweaked. You turn this dial, or that dial, and you fix the engine. A crime scene is a different kind of problem. You don't show up at a crime scene and say "You know what? Let's just move forward; what's done is done." That's a preposterous response to a crime scene. At a crime scene, the goal of understanding is entirely for the larger sake of preventing this outcome in the future. You have to first look backwards:

Who did this?

How did this happen?

Who is the person that did this?

How do we help the person to whom this was done?[21]

Many organizations treat inclusion as an engine problem, taking swift but superficial action. Since organizations are obsessed with goals, they may set aggressive hiring or promotion targets, or they may commit publicly to a stretch goal like "Gender Parity by 2025" and shout it from the proverbial rooftops. What gets measured gets done, as the business saying goes. What can possibly go wrong?

Although hiring goals may be met, for example, what matters more long-term is if those who were hired actually stay, and if the culture is one in which they believe they can thrive. Peter Drucker's quote, "Culture eats strategy for breakfast," points out the power of culture to support or undo good actions and intentions, and it is especially true when it comes to creating an environment that feels welcoming for all. If you notice that you don't have a full pipeline of diverse talent to choose from, or that certain people are not staying, or team members are failing to perform, then you likely have an inclusion problem within your company's culture. If you treat inclusion like a crime scene instead of an engine problem, you'll be able to get to the root of the issue.

GET FEEDBACK: *To increase your self-awareness, it's important to seek feedback from others on how you are perceived. The easiest thing might be to tell a few of your colleagues that you're reading this book, and one of the exercises is to seek out feedback on your inclusiveness. Ask these team members if they think you prioritize inclusion in the workplace. Push to have them give you honest answers and examples. You may be delightfully surprised or devastated by their answers. Either way, it's important to know where you stand so you can better plan how to move forward.*

Next Steps

You've taken a huge step toward inclusive leadership by choosing to increase your awareness. We've talked about all the different kinds of knowledge you'll need—data, research, and stories—to add to your arsenal, and we've also talked about some of the emotions that arise when we are challenged with our own lack of understanding or incompetency.

There is a danger, particularly as leaders move into manager-level and senior roles, that they will become isolated from real-time knowledge and from honest conversations, feedback, and support. But inclusive leaders constantly listen to and gather feedback from those around them. In particular, they know to seek this information from those who are very different from themselves, ensuring that they are appropriately challenged, and not just in an echo chamber of their biggest champions.

At this stage, you should also be thinking seriously about the support you want to give others. In offering what you have that's easy to share based on your access or position or the acceptability or status that you have, you can earn the trust of those you seek to help and maybe even benefit from *their* support, further down the road. Good will is built this way, brick by brick, and by offering to give first, rather than first seeking to receive.

At this stage, it's great to do a pulse check. As you're learning more, what is making you feel like you want to take action? What has captured your mind and your heart? Maybe it's a particular community you belong to. Maybe you're newly committed to overcoming biases you only recently realized you had. Maybe you've realized you want to bring more of your true self to work, both for your own well-being and to role model to others what might be possible for them. All of these motivations will serve as fuel when you enter the next phase of the continuum: Active.

AS YOU WRAP UP THIS CHAPTER, TAKE A MOMENT TO REFLECT ON THE FOLLOWING QUESTIONS:

- To stay aware, I must dedicate myself to continuous learning—as all inclusive leaders do. How will I keep gathering new information and exposing myself to new perspectives?

- What will I begin to explore in my own story through courageous self-awareness?

- How will I remain vigilant for biases in everyday interactions? Do I feel comfortable calling them out, both in myself and others?

CHAPTER FOUR

Active

An individual has not started living until he can rise above the narrow confines of his individualistic concerns to the broader concerns of all humanity.

—MARTIN LUTHER KING, JR.

Bria Sullivan, a Google software engineer and tech advisor, describes the steps she took to make a difference in the tech industry. In June of 2018, she shared on Twitter the results of her plan, reporting, "Two months ago I made a promise to help ten Black adults get jobs in technical roles by the end of the year. As of today, three of them have accepted offers, totaling $450,000 in compensation!"[1]

Sullivan says she offered these individuals resume reviews, technical mentorship, mock interviews, and a lot of mental support. By tweeting her tangible action plan, Sullivan caught the attention of hiring managers in the tech world who were interested in interviewing her mentees who were still looking for a job. Since the tech industry is predominantly white, Sullivan ultimately helped bring more diversity to numerous companies in the industry. Her work made a real difference. She reflected on her ongoing effort to boost the careers of a few individuals, saying, "I ultimately hope that other people who see this will be inspired to do the same. We don't always need huge solutions that take a while to implement. You can start by a few people at a time. Don't give up on them."

Activating can also take place on your own behalf. A news story went viral in 2016 about how female cabinet members in President Obama's team strategically prepared to be heard.[2] They noticed that they were being overlooked during discussions, so they joined forces and developed a strategy called *amplification*. When a woman made a good point during a meeting, the other women repeated it and gave credit to the originator. This method brought attention to the women's contributions and prevented the men from taking credit for an idea that wasn't theirs—something that happens with surprising frequency in the workplace when certain voices are more dominant than others.

It may be tempting to give in to feelings of powerlessness when you acknowledge the sheer magnitude of effort required to move the needle, but as these stories demonstrate, gestures don't need to be grand to make a difference. It's easy to underestimate the power of small commitments enacted by single individuals when it comes to challenging systems.

My intent in sharing these stories is also to provide a wake-up call to the hard work being done by a few. Why should those who are being discriminated against be alone in their efforts to fix the situation, when there are many hands available to assist?

In the Aware stage of the Inclusive Leader Continuum discussed in the last chapter, you worked hard to learn and gain exposure to new stories you'd perhaps never considered before; in the Active stage, you have the opportunity to act on that knowledge. This choice is a big threshold, because it's the do-or-die moment for anyone who aspires to be considered an inclusive leader. It is the moment when you sign up to do more than is expected and to assume a new level of responsibility.

Marshall Goldsmith's book title rings true here: *What Got You Here Won't Get You There*.[3] Activation is about choosing a new road as well as leaving behind some unproductive behaviors that prevented you from taking action in the past. No matter who you are, you have the opportunity to help steer how change happens, to whom, and with whom. This chapter will help you develop your point of view on what needs to be challenged—in yourself, and in your organization—and how to challenge people and systems effectively.

In this stage, you're moving past feeling overwhelmed by the new knowledge you're accumulating so you can tackle the next challenge, which comes with its own obstacles. For example, in taking action, what if you do or say the wrong thing? What if you break trust instead of building it? These are all learnings and calibrations that will serve to strengthen you as an inclusive leader. At this stage, the resilience you develop is irreplaceable. It might be both nerve-wracking and exhilarating for you at the same time.

Where to Start?

The tricky thing about action is that you won't always get instant gratification. Leaders love short cuts and quick fixes. So much business jargon proves how obsessed we can be with "key takeaways" and "next steps." But action doesn't always work like that. Even if you're actively trying to drive change, you have to be patient rather than get discouraged. The same is true for people who want to progress quickly through the different stages in this book.

> *The tricky thing about action*
> *is that you won't always*
> *get instant gratification.*

No magic amount of time is spent at each step of the continuum, and this is perhaps never truer than at the Active stage. Using your voice and your platform to act effectively, with the desired impact, is a skill that you need to develop over time. Your personal journey toward becoming a more inclusive leader can span many years and involve difficult work. When you read leadership books, you don't expect to be transformed in a moment into someone who is immediately more skilled. That's why it's critical to be patient with yourself as you begin to activate.

This stage can feel overwhelming, but exciting too. What should you do first? Where should you activate, with whom, and for whom? The way you activate will be unique to you. Because you have a lot of choices, it's perhaps most important to consider where you are most comfortable and energized.

At first, you might find it easier to follow someone else's lead. Change cannot happen with a small number of hands doing the majority of the work. If you sense somebody must be exhausted from pushing the boulder uphill, consider how to chip in to give them a well-deserved break. Perhaps you can commit to learning as much as you can in your company's **Employee Resource Groups (ERGs)** or **Business Resource Groups (BRGs),** if they exist, about where your voice or your hands are needed most. This may help you understand a practical starting point for stepping up on behalf of others with whom you don't share an identity. For example, you don't have to identify as LGBTQ+ to help organize a PRIDE event at your organization.

The book *Lean In* has become a classic for many reasons.[4] Its core concept is to encourage women to engage in the same proactive way that male colleagues do in advocating for their career advancement. The challenge with this, though, was immediately clear. Women are already fighting an uphill battle when it comes to being welcomed, valued, respected, and heard in the workplace (and elsewhere). Perhaps in addition to women—and other underrepresented groups—leaning in, men need to lean back, making some additional room for women and meeting them halfway. A push and a pull, if you will. If seen through this lens, it's clearly a mutual commitment that's needed. A responsibility comes with this challenge to women, to show up differently, and it's a challenge to men to prepare the ground. It is paramount that anyone taking the risk to push more is not met with resistance. Sometimes it's as simple as opening a window in the conversation for someone else.

The ManBassador Bingo Card (see Figure 4.1) is a funny adaptation of a helpful graphic called the Tech Diversity Bingo Card.[5] The 3% Conference, an annual event to champion creative female talent and leadership, created this version to outline helpful behaviors male leaders in the creative industry can model to make room for their overlooked coworkers. For example, male inclusive leaders can **center** female coworkers by doing some of the following:

- Giving women the floor during discussions and not interrupting them when they're speaking

- Inviting women to sit at the table during conferences, instead of on the sidelines

- Amplifying female voices in meetings and on social media if they're not getting the recognition that they deserve

Figure 4.1. The ManBassador Bingo Card

Although some champions of inclusion would argue that companies should be far beyond needing this type of resource, I know—from my company's many consulting engagements—that many are not. I will say, however, that this bingo card should be modified and utilized by more than just men for women. Many of these concepts apply to multiple underrepresented or marginalized groups. The heart of the message is about actively supporting colleagues who haven't been afforded the same level of equity in the workplace, and that's a major takeaway at this stage in your journey.

Further, the small actions suggested on the card are simple things that anyone can do. If you haven't been very active in supporting diversity and inclusion at your organization, these steps are perfect for becoming active. In fact, if you can ultimately make these actions part of your new normal, you'll be miles down the road toward your journey of becoming an inclusive leader.

Over time, as you find your confidence growing, you'll find your actions become more visible and less hidden behind closed doors. You might even gear your actions to be noticed—like those of the 20,000 Google employees and contractors who took a calculated risk by walking out of the company's offices around the world, one week after the *New York Times* reported that Google had protected three executives accused of sexual misconduct.[6] Their collective action worked. In the immediate aftermath, Google eliminated forced arbitration in cases of sexual harassment and committed to more transparency in sexual harassment reporting. Of course, this result doesn't totally solve the issue, but employees' actions can force much-needed progress.

Mentoring and Sponsoring

Mentoring has always been a powerful tool for professional development and career advancement, especially when mentors go the extra mile to help mentees. The all-star mentors who put their own professional or social capital on the line for another person are often called **sponsors.** They advocate for their sponsees and talk them up when they are in the room and, more importantly, when they are not in the room. This kind of support is invaluable for some to get ahead.

However, this typically informal workplace system, like so many others, is ripe with unfairness; most mentor/sponsor relationships involve people who share the same identity, for instance.

If I were to ask you whom you mentor and whom you sponsor, would they look like you? When I ask senior leaders about their mentees, and those they sponsor intentionally, I often see male leaders with a majority of male mentees. This happens because those who have the confidence to ask for the support of an executive tend to hail from certain groups—those in the majority, who are well represented at the executive level—and not from others. Women, people of color, and other minorities who have historically been left out of the inner workings of an organization are also left out of these important relationships that could potentially help them advance.

Research has shown that building more intentional mentoring and sponsoring relationships, not just for women, but for all colleagues whose identity puts them outside the inner workings of an organization, has the most impact on improving representation challenges.[7] Sponsorship in particular creates the single biggest difference in the advancement of underrepresented talent.[8]

At this stage of your inclusive leader journey, you are ready to take greater actions, and mentoring/sponsoring is an excellent way to make an impact. Examine your mentee cohort and adjust accordingly if you currently only make time for those most similar to you. Examine your mentors and sponsors with the same lens. Be proactive in reaching out to less tenured colleagues from different backgrounds to let them know you are happy to provide advice and support. Don't assume they would feel comfortable coming to you without this invitation.

To take this a step further, encourage your company to formalize a mentorship/sponsorship program if you don't already have one. This will activate more people to help others, which will make it easier to have an impact on more employees who are underrepresented in the top rungs of the career ladder. But remember, the key is to prioritize mentor/mentee pairs that don't share the same demographics.

The reciprocal learning that can happen as a result of these mentoring relationships should not be underestimated. In other words, they don't only have to go one way. One creative mentoring scheme I've written about in a whitepaper featuring the Bank of New York Mellon is their Reverse Mentoring program, which includes pairs of executive mentees and Millennial mentors working for a year together on learning from each other.[9] You might assume this kind of mentoring of executives has to do with gaining more digital acumen from their Millennial leaders, but the conversations are much broader, touching on everything from how career pathing works in the company to younger talent's recommendations on emerging customer groups and ways to demonstrate company and social values more publicly. The program has spun off many new pairings and resulted in improved retention of the Millennial mentors and increased engagement from executive mentees as well.

Even if your company doesn't have a formal program—and most don't, yet—how can you construct a similar support network for your learning? It can be as simple as whom you surround yourself with, whose stories you read or listen to, and which circles you join.

The topic of how we support and mentor each other in a respectful way has become especially acute in the context of the #MeToo movement, which has shed light on damaging leadership behaviors and unfair workplace practices. Some research shows men are becoming more cautious in having the honest coaching conversations that women (and other diverse talent) so desperately need but haven't been able to have, historically.[10]

Instead of retreating in fear of mentoring colleagues who are more vulnerable than you, take special consideration of where and when mentoring occurs. Mentoring often occurs in casual conversations or informal social settings, after work or on weekends. An inclusive leader considers where a mentee might feel not only more comfortable, but also what time of day feels like the right professional setting for these important conversations. Do your mentoring in public places, and whatever you do, do it across the board. The need for safety is a universal one. When you are the one with the power, you have a responsibility to think three steps ahead for the comfort of others, regardless of your own identity.

> *When you are the one with the power, you have a responsibility to think three steps ahead for the comfort of others, regardless of your own identity.*

Lastly, becoming a mentor or sponsor is something that great leaders are doing already. Offering guidance and advice to less-tenured colleagues should not be extra work; it comes with the territory of being a effective leader. But to be an inclusive leader, you might need to think differently about how you offer support, and to whom.

Becoming the Storyteller: More Voices

Every way that you can notice your own victimization or the ways you've been marginalized, you can access the feelings other people might be having. Everybody has an experience of exclusion. Maybe it's not around a group identity; maybe it's just an individual experience, but there's power in recalling that and extrapolating it.

—VERNĀ MYERS

Stories are one of the most effective ways to educate and create the all-important aha moments that remain in people's minds. When told skillfully, they build a sense of connection between you and others and inspire people into action to bring about change, which is why they are particularly important for inclusive leaders. You may have often found yourself in the audience witnessing expert storytellers or hearing vulnerable shares by those who felt like they didn't belong. Which stories tugged on your heartstrings? You might remember your biases being interrupted by a surprising twist in someone's story that stopped you in your tracks. That's because effective stories often create **cognitive dissonance** for the listener; a personal belief is challenged by another viewpoint, which causes discomfort.

I take advantage of cognitive dissonance when I walk on stage as a diversity expert and also as a white woman whose sexual orientation is often inferred as straight. The truth never fails to surprise my audiences and is an opportunity for me to share my "why" more fully with some pivotal stories that drove me to do the work I do. For instance, if someone asks me what was (and is) my motivation for entering the diversity and inclusion space, I answer that I wanted to support more inclusive workplaces, because I know firsthand the pain of exclusion at work and all the potential that was thwarted in my professional path as a result of these dynamics. Some of this was imposed on me from a world steeped in bias and negative stereotypes about female leaders, of course, but some of it was also about my own limiting beliefs, inherited through messaging about my worth and my potential. I decided that I didn't want this toxic combination to continue to derail me or other talent from what we could achieve.

When you can identify the cognitive dissonance in your own story—a writer who has dyslexia; a former inmate turned youth advocate; a CEO who never finished high school—sharing it with others can help them overcome their own biases. When you can challenge people's biases by sharing your story, you're taking important action. Sharing your story around inclusion requires a certain willingness to expose some of the lessons you've learned on your journey—especially if you had to learn them the hard way—as well as your personal aha moments. Comfort with vulnerability is especially critical in showing your true self. It might feel risky or uncomfortable, particularly as you strive to present a strong face of certainty to your organization. But showing vulnerability does not, in fact, detract from a leader's capacity to inspire people; rather, it augments it.

> *Showing vulnerability*
> *does not detract from a leader's*
> *capacity to inspire people;*
> *rather, it augments it.*

Dr. Brené Brown's classic 2010 TED talk on vulnerability has approximately 36 million views and counting. It has become particularly popular in workplaces around the world as a leadership tool.[11] No one is perfect, yet it's become a norm in business to try to appear flawless, like we always have the answers. Not only is it a lot of work to maintain this image, it's also unrealistic and inauthentic. Leaders who show some vulnerability relate better with their colleagues and reports, coming across as more likeable. As vulnerability in the workplace is now becoming more widely practiced, now is the perfect time to share your personal story.

It used to feel risky for me to come out as LGBTQ+ over and over again—especially on stages in front of thousands of people. I continued to do it, however, and put aside my mood that day, or my sense of safety in that particular moment. Perhaps I was in front of an audience that I suspected wasn't going to appreciate that part of my identity, or I was speaking in a part of the world where, not only is a woman-expert anathema to the local culture, but certain sexual orientations are also literally criminalized.[12] But as I learned to activate myself, and practice authenticity in the moment, I grew comfortable with discomfort.

I became more confident in talking about my vulnerability, because I knew others would take my storytelling as a signal that I could see and hear and understand them, perhaps shifting something in their perception of themselves, or each other. I drew comfort from the thought that those audience members might, in my example, find the courage to share their own stories.

Tapping into Your "Why"

Your "why" begins to clarify at this point. By this I mean, why did you pick up this book and desire to be an inclusive leader in the first place? Given that the continuum and all the stages come with a lot of effort and commitment on your part, what in your own journey motivates you to remain committed to progress and your own growth? There is fodder in each of our experiences, and inclusive leaders mine their histories for instances small and large that illustrate compassion or hardships. Perhaps we tell stories about a loved one, or a valued colleague, whose journey made an impression on us.

In mining my own background, I never thought anyone would resonate with the story I mentioned earlier, of losing my voice during intense training as an opera singer and the hard journey of recovery. As I crafted that story into my first TEDx talk, I struggled with how to move through remembering and painting a picture for my audience of that very dark time into a larger conversation about why it might have happened. What began as a "Why me?" moment ultimately clarified my understanding of what I'm here to do. Life was redirecting me to use my voice—not as a singer, but to support others to find their voices and gain confidence in using them for the common goal of inclusion.

In our explorations as storytellers we should believe that every-thing (good, bad, and in between) happens for a reason and that part of our leadership journey is to excavate this meaning. Meaning might seem out of reach at first, but eventually it tends to materialize. But it will not do so without constant invitation.

Sharing personal stories is helpful for both readers and listen-ers. My personal story has taken on a different meaning for me over many years of telling it in keynotes all over the world. In processing it on stage and with the generous listening of audiences, I have healed from the devastation of walking away from my operatic dreams and have come to understand why things happened the way they did. The ways audiences have interpreted this story, as a metaphor for losing anything we value and fighting to turn adversity into strength, has turned out to be something that many can relate to.

If you are ready to investigate the structure of your story, I recom-mend the advice of Erin Weed, founder of Evoso and one of the most talented TEDx speaker coaches I know, about the arc of effective sto-ries, which is Story, Truth, and Universal Truth:

STORY

- What occurred?
- What action was taken?
- How did you change? What did you do differently?
- What changed as a result?

TRUTH

- What did you take from the learning?
- What has been the result over time?
- How do you know it was important or significant?
- What ultimate lesson did you take away?

UNIVERSAL TRUTH

- What can the audience take from your story?
- What can be learned or applied?
- What do you hope for, for others?

Universal truths can be many things, and as I indicated, they emerge over time, often with the help of your listeners or audiences. You can decide that you think you know the universal truth of a story, but conversations with various listeners can open your eyes to many new interpretations. Perhaps that conversation will shift how you tell the story and how you share it in the future.

Centering Underrepresented Storytellers

When talking about the power of stories, we can't ignore the way most people consume stories—through published media. To hear more diverse stories, we must seek out, support, and center different voices.

For example, when you think of industry experts, do they tend to be of a certain gender or ethnicity? In many fields, white men are overrepresented when it comes to publishing books, speaking at conferences, and being interviewed or cited in publications. What message do you think this may be sending to leaders who don't share the same identity? The impact of a lack of diverse storytellers is that underrepresented voices don't see themselves at the top and therefore feel their viewpoints aren't going to be valued in those circles. An inclusive leader can challenge all of this in concrete ways.

How many books have you read recently that were written by women, people of color, or other minority demographics? There are plenty of diverse authors to choose from. And you don't just want to read these books—you want to talk them up and share stories from them. These are simple ways you can be active about inclusion. Quote more less-quoted sources and their wisdom. Indicate that you value their point of view.

On the other side of the equation, you might have the opportunity to interrupt the status quo by sharing your own story. Your story is powerful, in its own right, but it can't work its magic if you never tell it. I've always loved the quote by Shirley Chisolm, the first African American woman elected to the US Congress: "If they don't give you a seat at the table, bring a folding chair."[13] You get to decide, at this stage, what you want to share, what feels important to voice, and what you believe may help shift others' perceptions or beliefs.

> *If they don't give you a seat at the table, bring a folding chair.*
>
> —SHIRLEY CHISOLM, the first African American
> woman elected to the US Congress

I am often one of the few women speakers on keynote stages and one of extremely few LGBTQ+ speakers. I take note of the diversity represented on stage among my fellow speakers. A main reason for the frequent uniformity of speakers is that those making decisions about who gets the platform aren't knowledgeable about, or don't prioritize, the need to center stories and storytellers from different communities. I hear resistance to "quotas" or chafing at the idea that more diverse speakers are needed, and most of all, I hear that diverse voices can't be located. To combat this resistance, some of my fellow speakers have stepped up. Some of the most impressive actions I have witnessed have come from speakers who have chosen to delegate their "seat" to others who could add unique perspectives, suggesting a wide array of available female speakers, say, in the tech ecosystem.[14]

An inclusive leader tackles the issue of representational diversity at every opportunity, including by monitoring voices in their everyday lives. They show up honestly and transparently and notice who else is in the room and who else's voice may not be being heard. They know when to nominate others, when to step aside, and also, given the right circumstances, when to step forward and show leadership courage through storytelling, themselves. There is no one right answer, and it is a judgment call; the goal for an inclusive leader at this stage is to be sensitive to these dynamics in the first place.

GET FEEDBACK: *At this stage in the journey, you've been taking some concrete actions, and it's important to get feedback on your work. Circle back with colleagues who have seen your efforts to support diversity and inclusion and ask how those efforts have come across. Have you been helpful? Is there anything you could do differently next time? Getting this feedback is important for understanding whether you're using your voice effectively. At this point, it's also smart to connect with colleagues who are a little further along on the Inclusive Leader Continuum so they can share their wisdom with you.*

Next Steps

In this chapter, I defined what it means to be active as an inclusive leader: begin to act from your knowledge, ask for feedback and adjust your actions, look for additional ways to engage, and use your voice more publicly in the process. I talked about the role of storytelling and how to find the balance between centering the unheard stories of others, and stepping up and being vulnerable, yourself.

AS YOU LOOK TO MOVE FROM BEING ACTIVE TO BEING AN ADVOCATE—THE NEXT STEP OF THE INCLUSIVE LEADER CONTINUUM—ASK YOURSELF THESE QUESTIONS TO HELP DURING THIS TRANSITION:

- Who am I giving support to as I activate?
- How might I support others who need my voice?
- Can I activate for a different community or identity in need of allies?

For the rest of your journey as an inclusive leader, you will always be activating. You will constantly need to learn new information, tell new stories, seek feedback, adjust your approach, and support different communities. That means that you will revisit this stage often, even as you progress further as a leader. In the next chapter, we'll discuss how you can focus your activation efforts toward a particular group or purpose and therefore disrupt the status quo as an advocate.

As you're learning how to prioritize inclusion, remember to stay open and adjust your approach, whenever necessary. Stay focused on moving forward, but don't become impatient if the pace of change isn't as fast as you'd hoped. Inclusive leadership can be uncomfortable, like learning a new language, and progress does not always mean perfection.

CHAPTER FIVE

Advocate

You do not have to be me in order for us to fight alongside each other. I do not have to be you to recognize that our wars are the same. What we must do is commit ourselves to some future that can include each other and to work towards that future with the particular strengths of our own individual identities.

—AUDRE LORDE

Richard Jeanneret, the Americas Vice Chair and Managing Partner for the Northeast Region of EY, has made the journey from Unaware to Advocate with the help of his son, Henry, who came out as transgender in his senior year of high school. "As we experienced resistance from certain family members, I started to have that sort of epiphany moment—for the first time in my life as a heterosexual white male, [I felt] excluded. [I realized that] this must be on a very small scale [compared to] what LGBT people feel," said Jeanneret. When Henry came out as transgender, he wasn't allowed to use the boys' locker room or play on any of the boys' sports teams at his school. Henry says all of these things made him feel excluded, which fueled his motivation to advocate for transgender people. "I can't *not* be out because I need to advocate for myself and the countless other people like me who need their basic rights."

As Jeanneret saw his son go through such a challenging ordeal, his experience deeply affected how he viewed workplace equality issues. "As a leader, I moved from being inclusive to being more compassionate," said Jeanneret. "We could work with our LGBT group (at EY) not just as an affinity group, but as a real sponsor for our business; empowered to make a bigger impact for the business." Since then, he says he jumped in when it came to getting his senior colleagues at EY to understand how amending the civil rights legislation to protect LGBTQ+ professionals in the workforce was good for business.[1] When he had EY's support, he leveraged the power of this large firm to help ensure his voice was heard on a national level, speaking on Capitol Hill.[2]

Jeanneret is an example of a business leader turned powerful advocate. His level at EY helped him make real change, but this would not have been possible without his exposure to an advocate role model: his son. "The courage that he has shown . . . I can at least do these little things."[3]

This shows that you don't need senior-level status to spark change. As human beings, we are inspired by fearlessly authentic individuals of any age or professional level.

Ready for More

If you were in Jeanneret's situation and followed the same path, you would likely find yourself at the Advocate stage of the Inclusive Leader Continuum. Advocates are not only active in supporting others, they also interrogate norms and ask inconvenient questions, all with the goal of leveling the playing field at work and in life in general. This takes perseverance, bravery, and willpower. If you do this well, you can speed the path of many who are exhausting themselves in a system not built by them or for them. Advocates have the opportunity to ultimately reverse these dynamics, even if that's through one courageous action at a time.

Advocates know that many hands make lighter work, so they are strategic with how they make change happen and who needs to be involved. They spend time thinking about how to marshal commitment, build community, engage those in power and, in general, work smarter—not harder. They know that one-on-one work needs to be supported by institutional change, and they think about all the steps necessary to tackle this complex shift without overrelying on those already struggling to be heard. All of this takes the Active work described in the last chapter to the next level.

In a 2015 article for *The Guardian* about a rally in Harlem following the church shooting in Charleston, South Carolina, Features writer Rose Hackman captured the comments of Feminista Jones, a 36-year-old social worker and writer, who shouted into a bullhorn, "It's not about being on the outside and saying 'Yes, I support you!' It's about, 'Not only do I support you, but I am here with you. I am rolling up my sleeves. What do I need to do?'"[4] This is the energy that's needed at the Advocate stage. Michael Skolnik, civil rights activist and cofounder of The Soze Agency, affirms the importance of this mindset for advocacy: "[Instead of saying] 'You go first; I'll help you with your work,' we can say, 'Let's both go together.'"[5] Standing in solidarity with someone who may not benefit from the dominant systems that perpetuate inequality means looking critically at those systems, even if you are an "insider" who benefits from them.

Working alongside people in this way creates a reinvigorated sense of energy and accountability. I define an Advocate mindset as asserting, "I will identify systemic inequities in whichever organization I'm in, and if I can use my power and privilege to make lasting, sustainable change, then I'm going to do that." That is not to say that you can't engage if you don't believe you can make a difference; part of what matters is that you tried in the first place to do what is often the harder thing. Others will then have the benefit of having something to build on as a baseline.

At the same time, this does not mean you should make yourself the center of attention by taking over completely. A rallying cry for the disability rights movement gets this sentiment across: "Nothing about us without us."[6] In discussions pertaining to certain groups, seek out and listen to their perspectives first and learn where they need the most support, since it is their experience of exclusion that you're working to mitigate.

At the Advocate stage, you begin to question underlying facts, practices, and assumptions that perpetuate inequality. At this stage, inclusive leaders not only continue to support others one-on-one behind the scenes, but they also invite themselves into larger conversations that have the potential to create change of a different magnitude. This readiness and willingness to go bigger is a hallmark of the Advocate stage. As inclusive leaders travel the stages of the continuum gathering knowledge and applying new behaviors, many first activate in private settings—safe places where they can begin to experiment and find their voice. It's imperative for every inclusive leader to take that time to get feedback, calibrate, and ready themselves for a bigger role in the conversation, and perhaps in more public conversations, which they can then step into as advocates. That practice is the training, if you like, before the big match.

Advocates can be thought of as version 2.0 of the Active stage. Being an advocate requires you to use all of the tools available to you in order to tackle persistent issues that prevent others from thriving.

Here are some signs that you have arrived at the Advocate stage of the continuum:

- You think the status quo is intolerable and are unafraid to ask "why?"

- You are vigilant and educated enough to notice when colleagues are not feeling valued.

- You are unafraid to have difficult conversations or challenge the beliefs and behaviors of others, but you are mindful of how to do this in a way that maintains trust.

- In taking action, you've learned through trial and error what resonates.

- You proactively seek feedback (and are not just open to it, but accept and respond to it—taking full responsibility for your words, actions, and impact).

- You commit time, resources, and any capital that you can access (professional, personal, social, etc.).

- You don't care about the limelight; some of your work happens privately and remains unheralded.

A Systems Lens

As an advocate, your work becomes about questioning protocols that organizations have built that perpetuate an unequal playing field. This systems approach is perhaps even more critical than one-off solutions like a single mentoring conversation in that it means addressing a root cause that could totally negate the need to address symptoms one by one. Being an advocate is an opportunity to move from the superficial, Band-Aid approach to something deeper that gets to the heart of the issue and has the potential to improve the experiences of many.

> *Being an advocate is an opportunity to move from the superficial, Band-Aid approach to something deeper that gets to the heart of the issue and has the potential to improve the experiences of many.*

Most processes that companies follow perpetuate bias because they've never been critically examined under a systems lens. Those who *can* do something about it are either unaware there's a problem, in denial that inequities exist, or throwing their hands up about the supposed complexity of fixing the problem. The gaps you see today are a result of many systemic failures that haven't been openly challenged and addressed, as well as individual behaviors that perpetuate biased outcomes. Your organization's leadership may suspect a larger and problematic trend is afoot, but that means little unless they are actively working to correct it.

It may seem like systems managed by people are basically unfixable because of the entrenched reality of bias. But advocates see the whole picture, interrupting the status quo regardless, because they accept the challenge of ensuring their organization doesn't continue to allow a harmful cycle to perpetuate. They affect what they can.

Advocates need to be mindful of strategically aligning their efforts, managing more stakeholders and audiences, and cozying up to the power structure (or perhaps they are in the power structure due to their organizational role). If you *are* the power structure, even better. CEOs, for example, can make one big commitment as an advocate that both addresses disparities and shifts the systems behind those disparities.

In 2015, Salesforce conducted an investigation into possible unequal pay practices within their company. In a 2018 *60 Minutes* interview, the CEO, Marc Benioff, described how he was in denial about the preponderance of pay inequity at Salesforce when their chief of personnel, Cindy Robbins, first raised the issue. "I said, 'That's not possible here because we have a great culture. We're a 'best place to work.'"[7] Like many executives, Benioff wanted to see himself, and his leadership, in the best light.

But the hard numbers painted a different picture. Benioff says they soon found evidence of a gender pay gap everywhere: "It was through the whole company, every department, every division, every geography." The audit was a wake-up call for Benioff, and he immediately began making sweeping changes to address this inequality. He increased pay for women who were earning less than men for the same work, which cost Salesforce $3 million.[8] He also instituted a new general practice rule: he wouldn't hold a meeting unless 30 per cent of the participants were women. You can see how this kind of policy would quickly draw attention to roles and teams where women were underrepresented.

Benioff's reckoning with serious systemic issues within his own company is a perfect example of high-profile advocate work. He was made aware of an issue and created solutions that addressed it, even at a substantial cost to the company. And, equally importantly, he shared his company's imperfections publicly so others could witness the facts, his response, and the solutions implemented. He set a new bar.

Sustainable Advocate-level work requires consistency and vigilance. A second audit a year later showed that the gender pay gap had widened again, as Salesforce had acquired dozens of smaller firms that brought with them their unfair pay practices.[9] To address this, once again, Benioff equalized salary differences, spending another $3 million.[10]

Since then, Salesforce has committed to conducting regular equal-pay assessments. As Benioff acknowledges, "We're going to have to do this continuously. This is a constant cadence." He hits the nail on the head in describing effective Advocate work: one grand gesture may be just the start, with many more needed. Inclusive leaders at this level constantly reevaluate established systems to identify possible areas of improvement. With each audit, Salesforce identifies new factors to consider and fixes the points of failure—not just to solve that one particular instance, but so the problem itself disappears.

Most recently in 2018, Salesforce spent another $2.7 million on closing pay gaps to adjust the salaries of 6 percent of its global 30,000-person workforce, as reported by *Inc.*[11] This salary adjustment also addressed a pay gap in race in the US that was uncovered by the audit. Salesforce may consider additional strategies, because their annual assessments show the wage gap tends to reappear without constant scrutiny. However, the percentage of employees who needed adjustments decreased 45 percent from 2017 to 2018, which shows their strategy is working to make serious progress.[12]

You can see how taking this kind of impactful action is harder without having the decision-making power of a CEO, but ideas for change often come from an organization's general employee population and, in certain progressive workplaces, cascade upward to decision-makers. The Advocate stage is about spotting flaws in a system or process where bias intrudes. You can do this and become an advocate for change at any level within your company. You can examine any of the following workplace systems to see how bias affects outcomes:

- Meetings
- Sourcing talent
- Interviews
- Onboarding
- Performance reviews
- Promotion processes
- Succession management

Each of these workplace systems has numerous best practices for making them more inclusive. As an advocate, you will need to put in the work to research possible solutions, making sure to partner with colleagues who can offer support.

As an example, studies have shown that job postings can naturally attract mostly male or female applicants depending on the wording. Having *ninja* in a job posting has been shown to repel women just as calling an environment *supportive* or *collaborative* dissuades men from applying.[13] These kinds of words are typically seen as either more masculine or feminine, deterring people from applying when they don't match the implied stereotype. As an inclusive leader, you can advocate for analyzing your job postings to check for biased language. This could be a huge step forward in building a pipeline of highly qualified, diverse candidates. Many tools and technologies are being designed to help uncover and fix biased systems, such as Textio Hire, which can scan your job postings for words that have been shown to alienate certain demographics.

Far from being powerless, advocates at every level of a company know how and when to ask powerful questions and to question norms as well as move conversations toward more public commitments to change.

> *Far from being powerless, advocates at every level of a company know how and when to ask powerful questions and to question norms as well as move conversations toward more public commitments to change.*

The Messenger Matters

Inclusive leaders at the Advocate level consider diversity at all levels, in every gathering or format, and are especially aware of the sometimes-outsized impact of a single action, delivered in their particular voice.

Robin DiAngelo, a white woman and a race educator, is currently speaking to primarily white audiences around the country about racial bias and how white people participate (unwittingly, for many) in oppressive systems built to favor their identity.[14] Robin's family history is one of extreme poverty; though she was aware of her class **oppression** growing up, she wasn't always aware of her racial privilege as a child. Her 2018 book, *White Fragility,* stems from her commitment to helping white people develop racial literacy, particularly at a time when many feel hesitant to confront racism but are awakening to the need to confront it in more concrete ways. She has decided the message is too important to be fearful of audience reactions, hate mail (which she receives), and other defensive or violent reactions.

She has all the hallmarks of someone at the Advocate stage who is using her privilege to get into rooms, speak to audiences, and do all that she can to interrupt the status quo, effectively placing herself on the front lines, among members of her own community of identity.

In the story that opened this chapter, Richard Jeanneret, a **cisgender** (a person whose identity corresponds with their birth sex) white male, shared identities with the majority of senior executives in his company. He chose to advocate for transgender people, a group that has been consistently stereotyped, misunderstood, and discriminated against. In becoming an advocate, he leveraged the privileged aspects of his identity to get the attention of his cisgender colleagues who were perhaps unaware of the struggles transgender people face in the workplace. Although he was coming from a place of privilege, he took risks with how other people saw him by becoming so vocal. His message ultimately spread so widely because of his status as a senior leader.

With practice, you can develop your own ability to perceive who's in the room and who's not, who's being heard and who's not, and you can act to educate the people around you—giving them a chance to learn and grow and develop their *own* sensitivity to inclusion and exclusion dynamics. Although those with relatively more privilege at the Advocate level may still get pushback, they will usually get less of it. Although all messengers need to be prepared with arguments, language, and a heavy dose of patience, identity will impact whether and how you are heard.

Ray Arata, the founder of the Better Man Conference, realized early on that he could best be an advocate as a man by addressing the often-unseen privilege within his own identity group. Author Jack Myers ascribes this unseen privilege to "the history of men who haven't needed help. They have grown up in a world where man was the master of the domain. So why even think about this because it's not an issue? We have other priorities."[15] Arata's conference has attracted hundreds of men who *are* aware that they have a role to play, and who come together to discuss their role in building more inclusive organizations.[16] These men have an incredible opportunity to activate and role model advocacy to others back at the office, later on.

> *You may risk ostracization from your in-group because you are telling the truth and breaking a code that protects them.*

Weathering the Storm

Pushing to address root causes and biased practices does not come without risk. And risk goes up when you become more public, moving from awareness, to action, to advocacy. As you make visible what has been hidden or protected, you create public accountability by beginning a conversation, which is a good thing. But anticipating the road ahead is important. You may risk ostracization from your in-group because you are telling the truth and breaking a code that protects them. People may accuse you of having biases for particular groups, question your motives, or go out of their way to point out your flaws. Even when you're trying to help people and evoke positive change, some people will have a negative reaction. It's important to anticipate pushback so you aren't blindsided by people who aren't as far along on their journey to becoming inclusive leaders.

When I decided to name our initial stage of the Inclusive Leader Continuum "Unaware," I knew that sometimes the nature of this stage goes beyond unawareness to apathy, antipathy, antagonism, and even anger. As an advocate, you will lock horns more often with those who are at the earlier stages of their own journeys and sometimes you'll meet with all of these reactions (and sometimes, if you're very lucky, simultaneously!). A phenomenon has been identified for this type of pushback: **identity protective cognition** is a documented phenomenon in which individuals who encounter new information that is inconsistent with their beliefs and cultural identity tend to dismiss or diminish that information.[17] They do so to protect their sense of self and the social position of the affinity group they belong to.[18] Truth can be a direct challenge to identity.

Take social media, for example, which is an increasingly popular forum for disseminating information. Voices on Twitter that spread messages of inclusion and education about bias are routinely harassed or **trolled**. Those in a majority identity pay a price for stepping outside of that system to challenge others, but female voices, people of color, and others who find themselves pushed to the sidelines who share their personal experiences online often experience much more extreme criticism. There's a constant push and pull between those willing to educate others and hostile audiences who are unreceptive to different perspectives, and who are very public about it. When you challenge biases, you need to stay strong and resilient, even when it feels like you aren't making much progress. The amazing thing about becoming more public with your inclusion work is that vast communities are ready to defend individuals who are being mistreated. This swarm of defense can happen as quickly as harassment can, especially on social media.

*Truth can be a direct
challenge to identity.*

How can we, as advocates, protect ourselves, as well as others, in doing the important work at this stage? Here are some ideas for getting the support you need to use a bigger voice while mitigating whatever risk you can:

MAKE THE BUSINESS CASE   When possible, connect your case for change to business drivers for those who have power and influence. This embeds new ideas in an argument that many can understand. Why is change critical? What message is important to send with an action, and to whom? Why does it matter to the viability of the business or organization? How many dollars are on the line if we don't get this right?

IDENTIFY AND ALIGN CHAMPIONS   Line up your champions and do so strategically. These should be a combination of those with official seniority in your company and those with social capital, too; when it comes to challenging norms around workplace culture, it is important to demonstrate a cross-identity coalition of those who believe in your ideas and who will step forward to support (or work behind the scenes to socialize) your efforts.

TEND TO SELF-CARE AND PERSONAL SUSTAINABILITY   In his TEDx talk, psychologist Guy Winch discusses the importance of emotional hygiene: the practice of taking care of your mind with the same diligence with which you take care of your body.[19] As an advocate, you will often feel like you are fighting an uphill battle, and this stress can affect your emotional health. Winch suggests a few actions in these moments of crisis:

- When in emotional pain, treat yourself with the same compassion you'd expect from a truly supportive friend rather than with self-criticizing behavior.

- Resist the urge to ruminate on failures. Instead, learn from them and quickly move on in order to protect your self-esteem.

- Develop emotional resilience by battling negative thinking, consciously adopting a positive mindset and reaching out for help when you need it.

It's also incredibly smart to get keyed in to the difference your work is making for others. This will reconnect you with a sense of purpose. For example, I often get heartfelt messages from audience members after my keynote speeches. People thank me for sharing my story and for being a voice for LGBTQ+ people. This goes a long way toward giving me extra fuel and stamina to keep going. I make it a priority to really take this kind of positive feedback to heart, and I recommend you do the same.

If you've been working hard and haven't received a lot of personal feedback, don't be afraid to check in with your team members and ask how they think you've been doing. Chances are, you're helping more than you realize. A delightful surprise for many who step into the Advocate stage is an expanded or unexpected community of new colleagues and friends who share a passion for change. With a more public platform, advocates get noticed, and others take a cue from their courage, the battles they choose to fight, and the stories they disclose. Many helpers and fellow travelers will materialize, and we can look back at this stage of our journey and remark on how transformational these new relationships can be.

Next Steps

Leaders should be uncomfortable if they're leading in the right way. At the Advocate stage in our inclusive leader journey, you'll find yourself ready to be uncomfortable, as often as necessary, with the discipline to continue learning, the resilience to withstand resistance, and the stamina to continue to analyze old problems in new ways.

GIVEN THE MYRIAD ARENAS THAT NEED THE HELP OF ADVOCATES, HERE ARE SOME QUESTIONS TO CONSIDER AS YOU CONTINUE TO BECOME A MORE INCLUSIVE LEADER:

- What do I notice in my organization, at the systems level, that I can challenge?

- How can I be more public in how I advocate for change?

- Where do I feel especially safe challenging processes, people, and biases at work? Do I have special access or influence that others do not? How could I use those advantages?

- What type of risk am I willing to take in order to advocate for others?

- Who has my back and is in my support system should I need them?

- How will I proactively take care of myself, so I can continue my journey of advocacy?

CHAPTER SIX

Stay Committed
to the Journey

With the historical focus on marginalized groups, we've been treating
diversity and inclusion as if we'd focus only on crunches to prepare for a
marathon—when really the entire body needs to prepare for the endeavor.
We need to strengthen all the muscles of the body to take that leap
forward.

—TIA SILAS, VP, CHIEF DIVERSITY AND INCLUSION OFFICER, IBM

If you think back to the story I shared in the Introduction where I was
hired to lead an inclusion training for twenty-five white male executives who didn't want to be there, maybe you now have a different
perspective on all of the things that might have led to that moment.
Chances are, biases permeated that company's culture countless times
over the years, from long-standing systems and processes to harmful
actions from individuals.

Don't get me wrong—I didn't think those executives were bad
people then, and I still don't. But I *do* think the vast majority of
people in charge at that organization were in the Unaware stage

of the Inclusive Leader Continuum. They probably had no idea what their non-male, non-white colleagues were going through at work, since the experience was vastly different from their own reality. And since they didn't understand the problem, they weren't able to take the brave and necessary leadership actions that could have helped the company correct course and prevented the behavior that called for discrimination and harassment lawsuits.

Many organizations find themselves in similar situations, and many more are well on their way to a breaking point if they don't make meaningful changes soon. The reality is that biases have permeated just about every aspect of the professional world, from decades (if not centuries) of pattern build-up. This is not a problem that will just go away if we all think good thoughts.

Don't Forget

If you only remember one thing from this book, remember that to be an inclusive leader, you need to *do something*. Good intentions are not enough. Change is about action. And if you aren't taking action, your silence is a passive acceptance of the status quo, which further perpetuates the problem.

> *If you only remember one thing from this book, remember that to be an inclusive leader, you need to do something.*

Assuming responsibility sounds like a simple thing, but social psychology tells us otherwise. As human beings, we are hardwired to believe that someone else will step in and do the hard work so that we don't have to. In fact, the more people who witness an injustice, the less likely people are to step forward and help. This is called the **diffusion of responsibility.** The term became mainstream after the 1964 rape and murder of Kitty Genovese in New York City, when a reported 38 people heard or saw her attack, but no one called the police or tried to intervene. Apparently, everyone assumed someone else would help. When news of this tragedy spread, the world was baffled that so many people could have stepped in to save Genovese's life but didn't.

Understanding why this crime wasn't stopped is important for us to comprehend why all kinds of injustices are allowed to continue. We falsely believe that our need to intervene decreases as the number of witnesses increases. In a world that's more connected than ever before, this reality further complicates an already complex problem. When we hear about injustices through the media, social media, or through the grapevine at work, it's easy to assume it's someone else's fight. But it's not. If it were always someone else's fight, no one would ever be there to do the work. We need to acknowledge that this is a flawed way of thinking, and it's time for us all to move past it.

A New Perspective

This book has likely given you a new perspective when it comes to all kinds of issues in the workplace—and outside of it. You might feel like an advocate on behalf of some people but like you're still moving out of unawareness when it comes to others. That's totally natural. Remember that the Inclusive Leader Continuum is not a linear journey, and you must be patient with your progress. You may travel forward and backward in your level of understanding and advocacy, but the important thing is that you are committed to the journey.

As someone who has made inclusion my life's work, I still regularly expose myself to new ideas, new voices, and new strategies for working toward equality. I travel through the continuum regularly, which keeps me humble and even more aware of how much work is to be done. When I encounter people who aren't as far along on their journey, I do my best to reach back through the continuum and try to pull them from unawareness to awareness all the way to advocacy.

Oftentimes all this work takes a lot of effort. It's hard not to feel fatigued and frustrated and wonder if I'm making a difference. On my own journey, it's been essential for me to find and harness my motivation so I don't give up when times are hard. It's funny because, even in hostile training situations like the one I described earlier, where I can see very little diversity in the room, someone will sneak by me at the end of a session and quietly say, "thank you." *That's* how I know I need to keep going. That person may not have had the courage to speak up much in the meeting, but they appreciated my voice.

Human potential is unleashed
when we feel like we belong.

As you work to figure out what keeps *you* motivated, I urge you to stay connected with the meaning behind supporting inclusion. I deeply believe that getting work done together has always been about feeling included. Human potential is unleashed when we feel like we belong. This goes beyond what we functionally "know" and "do"—our job tasks and deliverables. Yes, we want to shine for these, and be acknowledged, but we also want to trust that others will see—and seek out—our uniqueness; that they'll view it as a positive, and not be biased against our difference. We also want to feel our commonality with others—a sense of community, of sharing experiences in common, of feeling less alone. These things are worth fighting for, even when it's hard.

The qualities that make us different are far from irrelevant; they are core to who we are, why we do what we do, and how we get our energy. We do better work when we feel like the different aspects of our identity are celebrated and we belong. Difference—when met with inclusive behaviors—enables higher-quality problem solving through *creative abrasion,* where ideas are productively challenged, avoiding the dangers of groupthink. This is the magic behind great organizations; employees who feel valued create more valuable organizations that are able to innovate, to pivot, to calibrate, to anticipate and respond, and to care.

As a leader, you can do a seemingly endless number of things to support a more inclusive environment where everyone can thrive. Even when you feel like you're powerless—just one person in a huge organization—or you have little decision-making power, or you're up against deeply entrenched biases, you can still make a difference with your own actions. The desire to feel welcomed, valued, respected, and heard on a daily basis is universal. When you fill that need for your coworkers, it will not go unnoticed.

Throughout my many years of working with professionals to create more inclusive and equitable workplaces, I've noticed that the most beloved leaders consider themselves students. They humble themselves and keep stepping into new conversations, spaces, and skill sets. They practice what's uncomfortable, proactively gaining exposure and new networks so that they can learn and grow. And rather than believing they have nothing to contribute when it comes to diversity and inclusion, they recognize that they are part of the solution. Although they might not have all the answers on how to make an impact, they empower themselves to keep learning.

I wrote this book to help individuals better understand how they can make small changes that create resounding impact—no matter what their title or industry or how far along the continuum they find themselves. But personal courage and transparency must be met halfway at the organizational level, in the form of colleagues, managers, and leaders. It's a two-way street. The environment we create can activate *a new level of authenticity* in the workplace. If we "leap," the net *must* appear to catch us. We need each other, more than ever, to capture the promise of inclusion and make it a reality. As the fight for inclusion gains even more momentum, I believe we'll reach a critical mass when things will start to change exponentially. The wheels are already in motion and, if we continue to focus on unity, I believe we're in for amazing changes.

I've noticed that the most beloved leaders consider themselves students.

As this book comes to an end, remember that inclusion is a daily practice. And as with any habit, change takes practice. I look forward to witnessing the fruits of your efforts to create workplaces where everyone has opportunities to thrive.

Notes

Introduction

1. William Fey, "Diversity Defines the Millennial Generation," Brookings: The Avenue, June 28, 2016, *https://www.brookings.edu/blog/the -avenue/2016/06/28/diversity-defines-the millennial-generation/*.

2. Juliet Bourke, Stacia Garr, Ardie van Burkel, and Jungle Wong, "Diversity and Inclusion: The Reality Gap," Deloitte, February 28, 2017, *https:// www2.deloitte.com/insights/us/en/focus/human-capital-trends/2017 /diversity-and-inclusion-at-the-workplace.html*.

3. Cristian Dezsö and David Ross, "Does Female Representation in Top Management Improve Firm Performance? A Panel Data Investigation," *Strategic Management Journal*, 9, January 13, 2012, *https://onlinelibrary .wlley.com/doi/abs/10.1002/smj.1955*.

4. Ariel Schwartz, "Here Are All the Quantifiable Reasons You Should Hire More Women," *Fast Company*, April 2, 2014, *https://www.fastcompany .com/3028227/here-are-all-the-quantifiable-reasons-you-should-hire -more-women*.

5. Chad Jerdee, "Getting to Equal: The Disability Inclusion Advantage," Accenture, *https://www.accenture.com/us-en/company-persons-with-disabilities* (accessed October 29, 2018).

6. Vivian Hunt, Lareina Yee, Sara Prince, and Sundiatu Dixon-Fyle, "Delivering Through Diversity," McKinsey & Company, January 2018, *https:// www.mckinsey.com/business-functions/organization/our-insights /delivering-through-diversity* (accessed October 29, 2018).

Chapter 1

1. Deloitte, "Uncovering Talent: A New Model of Inclusion," Deloitte, January 1, 2018, *https://www2.deloitte.com/content/dam/Deloitte/us /Documents/about-deloitte/us-uncovering-talent-a-new-model-of -inclusion.pdf.*

2. Maya Allen, "22 Corporate Women Share What Wearing Their Natural Hair to Work Means," *Byrdie,* August 21, 2018, *https://www.byrdie.com /natural-hair-in-corporate-america.*

3. Tara Hastings, interview with author, Fall 2018.

4. R.L.G., "How Black to Be?" *Economist,* April 10, 2013, *https://www .economist.com/johnson/2013/04/10/how-black-to-be.*

Chapter 2

1. Tarana Burke, "I was made aware of this video BEFORE I ever saw it because Tony Robbins people reached out to do damage control within 24 hours." Twitter, April 7, 2018, *https://twitter.com/taranaburke/status/ 982581323729694720?lang=en.*

2. Tony Robbins, "At a recent Unleash the Power Within (UPW) event in San Jose, my comments failed to reflect the respect I have for every-thing Tarana Burke and the #MeToo movement has achieved," Face-book, April 8, 2018, *https://www.facebook.com/TonyRobbins/posts/ at-a-recent-unleash-the-power-within-upw-event-in-san-jose-my -comments-failed-to/10156469713679060/.*

3. Catalyst, "Why Diversity and Inclusion Matter," Catalyst Inc., August 1, 2018, *https://www.catalyst.org/knowledge/why-diversity-and-inclusion -matter.*

4. Jennifer Brown, "Sports, Stereotypes and Sexual Orientation: Les-sons from a Gay ex-NFL Player," Jennifer Brown, Speaker, Author, Humanist, July 13, 2018, *https://jenniferbrownspeaks.com/2018/07/13 /sports-stereotypes-and-sexual-orientation-lessons-from-a-gay-ex-nfl -player/.*

5. Sam Sifton and Grant Barret, "The Words of the Year," *New York Times*, December 18, 2010, *https://www.nytimes.com/2010/12/19/weekinreview/19sifton.html*.

6. Kim Goodwin, "Mansplaining, Explained in One Simple Chart," BBC, July 29, 2018, *http://www.bbc.com/capital/story/20180727-mansplaining-explained-in-one-chart*.

7. Catalyst, "List: Women CEOs of the S&P 500," Catalyst, *https://www.catalyst.org/knowledge/women-ceos-sp-500* (accessed October 12, 2018).

8. Chuck Shelton. Interview with author, Fall 2018.

9. Wikipedia Contributors, "Illusory Superiority," last updated March 5, 2019, *https://en.wikipedia.org/wiki/Illusory_superiority*.

10. Kathryn Patricia Cross, "Not Can, But Will College Teaching Be Improved?" *New Directions for Higher Education* 17 (1997): 1–15.

11. Alexis Krivkovich, interview by author, August 18, 2017.

12. Bernard T. Ferrari, "The Executive's Guide to Better Listening," *McKinsey Quarterly*, February 2012, *https://www.mckinsey.com/featured-insights/leadership/the-executives-guide-to-better-listening*.

13. Mike Robbins, *Bring Your Whole Self to Work: How Vulnerability Unlocks Creativity, Connection, and Performance* (Carlsbad, CA: Hay House Inc., 2018), 57.

14. Amy Sun, "Equality Is Not Enough: What the Classroom Has Taught Me about Justice," *Everyday Feminism*, September 16, 2014, *https://everydayfeminism.com/2014/09/equality-is-not-enough/*.

15. Barbara Adams, "Viewpoint: The Myth of Meritocracy," Society for Human Resource Management, August 27, 2018, *https://www.shrm.org/hr-today/news/hr-magazine/0918/pages/the-myth-of-meritocracy.aspx*.

16. Sun, "Equality Is Not Enough."

17. Shelley Levitt," Why the Empathetic Leader Is the Best Leader," *Psychology Today*, March 15, 2017, *https://www.success.com/why-the-empathetic-leader-is-the-best-leader/*.

Chapter 3

1. Christie Smith and Kenji Yoshino, "Uncovering Talent: A New Model of Inclusion," Deloitte, *https://www2.deloitte.com/content/dam/Deloitte /us/Documents/about-deloitte/us-uncovering-talent-a-new-model -of-inclusion.pdf* (accessed October 23, 2018). Elliott Kozuch, "HRC REPORT: Startling Data Reveals Half of LGBTQ Employees in the U.S. Remain Closeted at Work," Human Rights Campaign (HRC), June 25, 2018, *https://www.hrc.org/blog/hrc-report-startling-data-reveals-half-of -lgbtq-employees-in-us-remain-clos*.

2. Paul Browde and Murray Nossel, "The Power of Two: How Listening Shapes Storytelling," TEDx Talks, January 31, 2014, *https://www .youtube.com/watch?v=JvOriYNJ15E*.

3. Sian Ferguson, "Privilege 101: A Quick and Dirty Guide," *Everyday Feminism,* September 29, 2014, *https://everydayfeminism.com/2014/09/what -is-privilege/*.

4. Women's Theological Center (*www.thewtc.org*), "Examples of Socioeconomic Status ('Class') Privilege," *https://sites.lsa.umich.edu/inclusive -teaching/wp-content/uploads/sites/355/2017/08/Examples-of-Socioeconomic -Status-Privilege.pdf* (accessed March 17, 2019).

5. Daysha Edewi, "What Is Privilege?" *BuzzFeed,* July 4, 2015, *https:// www.buzzfeed.com/dayshavedewi/what-is-privilege*.

6. Meg Bolger, "Why I Don't Facilitate Privilege Walks Anymore and What I Do Instead," *Medium,* February 16, 2018, *https://medium.com/@MegB /why-i-dont-won-t-facilitate-privilege-walks-anymore-and-what-i-do- instead-380c95490e10*.

7. Meg BolgerSafe Zone Project, "Privilege for Sale," Safe Zone Project, *https://thesafezoneproject.com/activities/privilege-for-sale/* (accessed November 3, 2018).

8. Kathy Martinez, interview by author, January 18, 2018.

9. Wade Davis, interview by author, August 6, 2018.

10. Nicole Sanchez, "In the past few years, I've been in a position to lead inside companies…," Twitter, June 19, 2018, *https://twitter.com /nmsanchez/status/1009260622884757505*.

11. Daniel Montello, "The Measure of Cognitive Distance," *Journal of Environmental Psychology,* June 1999, 101–122, *https://www.sciencedirect.com/science/article/abs/pii/S0272494405800714.*

12. Kimberlé Crenshaw, "Demarginalizing the Intersection of Race and Sex: A Black Feminist Critique of Antidiscrimination Doctrine, Feminist Theory and Antiracist Politics," *University of Chicago Legal Forum* 140 (1989): 139–167.

13. Philip Patston, "The Greatest Obstacle to Diversity and Inclusion," October 18, 2017, *http://www.philippatston.com/blog/the-greatest-obstacle-to-diversity-and-inclusion/.*

14. Tiffany Dufu, "As I was recently explaining to a straight, white man on Twitter who felt bullied over an insensitive remark he made about women: We all have to bear the responsibility of our privilege," Facebook, July 23, 2018, *https://www.facebook.com/tiffanydufu/posts/529412697477857.*

15. Sabrina Barr, "Thin Privilege, Writer Explains Meaning in Twitter Thread," *Independent,* July 23, 2018, *https://www.independent.co.uk/life-style/thin-privilege-explained-discrimination-body-size-fat-shaming-cora-harrington-a8459761.html.*

16. Reshma Saujani, "Why We Should Ditch the 'Perfect Woman' Myth," CNN, July 23, 2018, *https://www.cnn.com/2018/07/21/opinions/abortion-fertility-miscarriage-stories-matter-saujani-opinion/index.html.*

17. Stacy Jones, "White Men Account for 72% of Corporate Leadership at 16 of the Fortune 500 Companies," *Fortune,* June 9, 2017, *http://fortune.com/2017/06/09/white-men-senior-executives-fortune-500-companies-diversity-data/.*

18. U.S. Equal Employment Opportunity Commission, "2014 Job Patterns for Minorities and Women in Private Industry," U.S. Equal Employment Opportunity Commission, *https://www1.eeoc.gov/eeoc/statistics/employment/jobpat-eeo1/2014/index.cfm#select_label* (accessed October 12, 2018).

19. Bureau of Labor Statistics, "Labor Force Statistics from the Current Population Survey," United States Department of Labor, January 18, 2019, *https://www.bls.gov/cps/cpsaat03.htm.*

20. Ben Bartenstein, "Half of the sources I quoted this year for @business were women. That's 337 in total, or about one a day. Unfortunately, it's an anomaly in journalism & something I've failed at miserably in the past," Twitter, December 27, 2018 *https://twitter.com/BenBartenstein /status/1078331704501305344*.

21. Eric Johnson, "Elites Like Amazon's Jeff Bezos Think They're Being Phil- anthropic. But They Could Do So Much More." *Recode,* October 3, 2018, *https://www.recode.net/2018/10/3/17930990/anand-giridharadas -winners-take-all-book-changing-world-kara-swisher-decode-podcast-jeff -bezos*.

Chapter 4

1. Bria Sullivan, "2 months ago I made a promise to help 10 Black Adults jobs in technical roles by the end of the year." Twitter, June 22, 2018, *https://twitter.com/bria_sullivan/status/1010245936218427392*.

2. Claire Landsbaum, "Obama's Female Staffer Came Up with a Genius Strategy to Make Sure Their Voices Were Heard," *The Cut,* September 13, 2016, *https://www.thecut.com/2016/09/heres-how-obamas-female -staffers-made-their-voices-heard.html*.

3. Marshall Goldsmith, *What Got You Here Won't Get You There* (New York: Hyperion Publishing, 2014).

4. Sheryl Sandberg, *Lean In* (New York: Knopf, 2011).

5. Better Allies, "Tech Diversity Bingo Card FAQ," Better Allies, January 1, 2015, *https://maleallies.com/faq/* (accessed November 26, 2018).

6. Shirin Ghaffary and Eric Johnson, "After 20,000 Workers Walked Out, Google Said It Got the Message. The Workers Disagree," *Recode,* November 21, 2018, *https://www.recode.net/2018/11/21/18105719 /google-walkout-real-change-organizers-protest-discrimination-kara -swisher-recode-decode-podcast*.

7. Howard Waitzkin, Joel Yager, Tassy Parker, and Bonnie Duran, "Men- toring Partnerships for Minority Faculty and Graduate Students in Mental Health Services Research," *Academic Psychiatry* 30, 3 (May 2006), 205–2017, *doi: 10.1176/appi.ap.30.3.205*.

8. Audrey J. Murrell and Mike Fucci, "Sponsorship: A Powerful Career Accelerator for Diverse Talent," *Huffington Post,* September 22, 2016, *https://www.huffingtonpost.com/audrey-j-murrell/sponsorship-a -powerful-ca_b_12136476.html.*

9. BNY Mellon's Pershing, "Reversing the Generation Equation: Mentoring in the New Age of Work," BNY Mellon, February 15, 2018, *https://www .pershing.com/perspectives/reversing-the-generation-equation-mentoring -in-the-new-age-of-work.*

10. #MentorHer, "Key Findings," LeanIn.org and SurveyMonkey, *https//leanin .org/sexual-harassment-backlash-survey-results* (accessed April 25, 2019).

11. Brené Brown, "The Power of Vulnerability," TED Talk, TEDxHouston, June 2010, *https://www.ted.com/talks/brene_brown_on_vulnerability ?language=en.*

12. Rosamond Hunt, "This Is the State of LGBTI Rights around the World in 2018," World Economic Forum, June 14, 2018, *https://www.weforum .org/agenda/2018/06/lgbti-rights-around-the-world-in-2018/.*

13. Shirley Chisolm, "Quote by Shirley Chisolm," Goodreads, *https://www .goodreads.com/quotes/7687067-if-they-don t-give-you-a-seat-at-the -table* (accessed November 5, 2018).

14. Robyn Cusworth, "No More Excuses for All Male Panels: Here's 50 of the Best Female Speakers," *The Drum,* January 10, 2018, *https://www .thedrum.com/opinion/2018/01/10/no-more-excuses-all-male-panels -heres-50-the-best-female-speakers.*

Chapter 5

1. Richard and Henry Jeanneret, "Out Leadership and PwC present 'Out to Succeed,'" Out Leadership, YouTube, June 22, 2018, *https://www .youtube.com/watch?v=TyaTwVsNL2w.*

2. Out Leadership, "PwC and Out Leadership Launch Unique New Study of LGBT+ Emerging Business Leaders," *Cision: PR Newswire,* April 30, 2018, *https://www.prnewswire.com/news-releases/pwc-and-out-leadership launch -unique-new-study-of-lgbt-emerging-business-leaders-300638618.html.*

3. Jeanneret, "Out to Succeed."

4. Rose Hackman, "'We Need Co-Conspirators, Not Allies': How White Americans Can Fight Racism," *Guardian,* June 26, 2015, *https://www .theguardian.com/world/2015/jun/26/how-white-americans-can-fight -racism.*

5. Alan Feuer, "Michael Skolnik Taps His Social Network to Fight for Civil Rights," *New York Times,* November 20, 2015, *https://www.nytimes .com/2015/11/22/nyregion/michael-skolnik-political-director-for-russell -simmons-fights-for-civil-rights.html?_r=0.*

6. Isabella Rosario, "'Nothing about Us without Us': Disability Activists Appose Brett Kavanaugh," *Medium,* September 7, 2018, *https://medium .com/@isabellarosario/disability-activists-oppose-brett-kavanaugh-for-u-s -supreme-court-8b40176061bf.*

7. Lila MacLellan, "Denial, Bargaining, Acceptance: Salesforce's CEO on His Reckoning with Equal Pay for Women," *Quartz at Work,* April 16, 2018, *https://qz.com/work/1253580/salesforce-ceo-marc-benioff-tells-60 -minutes-about-his-reckoning-with-the-gender-pay-gap/* (accessed October 20, 2018).

8. MacLellan, "Denial, Bargaining, Acceptance."

9. Crunchbase, "Salesforce > Acquisitions," Crunchbase Inc., *https://www .crunchbase.com/organization/salesforce/acquisitions/acquisitions_list #section-acquisitions* (accessed October 20, 2018).

10. Cindy Robbins, "2017 Salesforce Equal Pay Assessment Update," Salesforce blog, April 4, 2017, *https://www.salesforce.com/blog/2017/04 /salesforce-equal-pay-assessment-update.html?d=70130000000tP4G%20.*

11. Marcel Schwantes, "The CEO of Salesforce Found Out His Female Employees Were Paid Less Than Men. His Response Is a Priceless Leadership Lesson," *Inc.,* June 26, 2018, *https://www.inc.com/marcel- schwantes/the-ceo-of-salesforce-found-out-female-employees-are-paid- less-than-men-his-response-is-a-priceless-leadership-lesson.html.*

12. Cindy Robbins, "2018 Salesforce Equal Pay Assessment Update, Salesforce blog, April 17, 2018. *https://www.salesforce.com/blog/2018/04 /2018-salesforce-equal-pay-assessment-update.html.*

13. Carmen Noble, "How to Take Gender Bias Out of Your Job Ads," *Forbes,* December 14, 2016, *https://www.forbes.com/sites/hbsworking knowledge/2016/12/14/how-to-take-gender-bias-out-of-your-job -ads/#64211dee1024.*

14. Robin DiAngelo, PhD, "Critical and Racial Social Justice Education," *https://robindiangelo.com/* (accessed October 20, 2018).

15. Jack Meyers, interview by author, March 24, 2017.

16. Better Man Conference, *https://www.bettermanconference.com/* (accessed October 20, 2018).

17. Soraya Chemaly, "Why Don't 'Good Men' Believe Women?" *Medium,* October 15, 2018, *https://medium.com/s/powertrip/why-dont-good-men -believe-women-23be0ce607c9.*

18. Dan Kahan, "Misconceptions, Misinformation, and the Logic of Identity-Protective Cognition," *Cultural Cognition Project Working Paper Series,* No. 164, May 24, 2017, https://papers.ssrn.com/sol3/papers .cfm?abstract_id=2973067.

19. Guy Winch, "Why We All Need to Practice Emotional First Aid," TEDx-LinnaeusUniversity, November 2014, *https://www.ted.com/talks/guy _winch_the_case_for_emotional_hygiene/up-next?referrer=playlist-the _importance_of_self_care%3E.*

Glossary

This is by no means an exhaustive list of all the terms an inclusive leader should be familiar with, but they are arising with increasing frequency in diversity and inclusion conversations.

Active stage   In this stage an inclusive leader proactively works toward equity and equal opportunities supporting those with underrepresented or marginalized identities, backgrounds, and experiences. This stage is about doing more than expected, pushing outside of your comfort zone, and finding your voice.

Advocate stage   In this stage an inclusive leader becomes a voice capable of transforming biased systems and sparking meaningful, widespread, scalable, lasting change. This stage is hallmarked by performing brave public actions that challenge deeply rooted beliefs and practices and taking some calculated personal or professional risk to shift behaviors.

Ally   A person of one social identity group who stands up in support of members of another social identity group and who is willing to act to help end discrimination, amplify unheard voices, and protect the rights of all.

Aware stage   In this stage an inclusive leader realizes that the playing field is not level in the workplace or in other group or organizational contexts. This stage is about beginning to understand other people's perspectives and stories and working through your own stories and biases.

Business Resource Groups (BRGs)   See Employee Resource Groups.

Bystander   Someone who witnesses something taking place but does not participate or assume an active role. The bystander has the choice to call something/someone out for problematic behavior or passively let it continue.

Capital (social or professional)   Capital, in this context, refers to assets one person or entity has to put into play on another person or community's behalf.

Center   To prioritize a certain idea or topic or to give something an extra amount of attention. In a diversity and inclusion context, centering often means giving someone the space and voice they usually would not have access to.

Cisgender   When your gender identity aligns with the sex you were assigned at birth.

Code switching   The inclination to change how you speak or express yourself based on who you find yourself surrounded by, often to make them feel more comfortable at your own expense.

Cognitive dissonance   The mental or psychological discomfort that occurs when you are exposed to content that contradicts your beliefs, preconceived notions, or assumptions.

Confirmation bias   The tendency to seek or notice information that confirms your belief and to avoid or ignore information that contradicts what you already think.

Covering   The strategic downplaying/minimizing of a stigmatized identity in order to avoid negative perceptions, harassment, or adverse professional effects.

Deflections   Defensive and often unconscious reactions to being called out or asked to prioritize diversity and inclusion. These statements, borne out of unconscious biases, sidestep responsibility and accountability and leave the important work for someone else to do.

Diffusion of responsibility   A sociopsychological phenomenon where the more people there are who witness an injustice, the fewer there are who step forward and help.

Distance biases   The tendency to favor those of us who are closer in space and time.

Diversity dimensions   The categories of identity that inform our unique experiences, backgrounds, and self-understanding. These classifications include (but are not limited to) race, gender identity, ethnicity, sexual orientation, physical and mental ability, age, socio-economic status/class, religion, political ideology, veteran status, citizenship, education, and appearance.

Emotional labor   The often-unrecognized effort behind managing feelings, expressions, and demeanor while fulfilling the emotional requirements of a job. Usually, people exert emotional labor at work to interact with coworkers, customers, or superiors, or to maintain social relationships.

Employee Resource Groups (aka ERGs, affinity groups, Business Resource Groups [BRGs], or business network groups)   Voluntary, employee-led groups that foster a diverse, inclusive workplace by gathering people together who share common interests, backgrounds, or identity factors. Often these groups will be categorized by affinity or diversity dimensions, such as race, gender, and sexual orientation; they have broadened in recent years to include disabilities, generations, and veterans.

Equality Create fairness by providing everyone with the same resources, treatment, and support, regardless of the differences between individuals that may influence what they need to thrive.

Equity Create fairness by providing people with individualized resources, treatment, and support in order to compensate for differences between individuals. Equity acknowledges the privilege afforded to certain individuals and attempts to level the playing field.

Identity Protective Cognition A documented phenomenon in which individuals who encounter new information that is inconsistent with their beliefs and cultural identity tend to dismiss or diminish that information to protect their sense of self and the social position of the affinity group they belong to.

Intent versus impact The idea that the impact of an action, behavior, or statement is more important than the intent behind it. In other words, having good intentions does not necessarily matter if your actions unwittingly offend, hurt, or further marginalize/oppress someone else, since that effect is the ultimate result of the interaction. This concept allows us to better recognize how our intentions translate as actions and to adjust them accordingly.

Intersectionality Originated by feminist theorist Kimberlé Crenshaw, the complex interaction between different stigmatized identities such as race, class, and gender. This mindset acknowledges that these diversity dimensions often overlap and create unique dynamics.

Latinx A gender-neutral term for a Latina or Latino person.

LGBTQ+ An acronym for lesbian, gay, bisexual, transgender, and queer or questioning (someone who is uncertain of their sexual orientation). The plus stands for the inclusion of all and is an intentional way to represent different identities and experiences. It's also common to see the acronym LGBTQQIA+, which encompasses a clearer representation of lesbian, gay, bisexual, transgender, queer, questioning, intersex, and asexual and/or allied people. An umbrella term that is supposed to signify a unified community, each letter also represents a different community in its own right with its own stories, experiences, and challenges.

Mansplaining   The word originates from the behavior of men who underestimate the understanding of the person they are talking to—often a woman, in this context—because they believe themselves to be more knowledgeable. Mansplaining manifests as a man explaining something that the listener likely knows just as much about, if not more, than the explainer.

Mentoring   The activity of someone who advises you on your current role and what you need to do in order to progress through your career. A mentor provides support and advice but is less active in creating change for you compared to a sponsor.

Myth of Meritocracy   The notion that companies are structured to reward only the most talented individuals, overlooking the fact that privileged individuals benefit from social advantages not granted to those who have had to work harder to overcome stereotypes and other challenges in order to ascend the corporate ladder.

Oppression   The systemic, cultural, legal, or institutional disadvantages those in certain groups experience as established by a history that has excluded them from various spheres of access. Oppression typically combines institutional discrimination with personal bias and prejudice. Due to the intersectional nature of identity-based power, it is likely we have all experienced some form of oppression or feeling of otherness at some point in our lives.

Optics   The way in which an event, person, or organization will be perceived by the general public. In a diversity and inclusion context, optics refers to how business decisions will appear socially just and morally in line with the company's values.

Privilege   Cultural, legal, social, or institutional rights/advantages that select people have access to solely because of their social group membership. Almost everyone has some form of privilege that can be leveraged to support those without it due to the intersectional nature of identity-based power.

Privilege walk   An exercise in which participants stand in a horizontal line and step forward or backward based on questions read by the facilitator. These statements address privilege stemming from race, gender and gender identity, class, sexual orientation, ability, and more, with the intention of visually demonstrating the different advantages people have had throughout their lives.

Self-enhancement bias   The unconscious tendency to boost your self-esteem and overestimate your abilities, especially in situations of threat or failure.

Sponsor   Someone with power who recognizes your potential and actively advocates for your success on the corporate/organizational ladder. This person typically has enough social capital to make a difference in others' perception of your performance and in the opportunities you are offered.

Tokenize   The practice of doing something (for example, hiring a person who belongs to a minority group) only to prevent criticism and give the appearance of equality.

Trolling   The deliberate act of making controversial comments to provoke unsuspecting victims who hold a contrary viewpoint to an argument online.

Unaware stage   In this stage an inclusive leader does not notice or understand that certain demographic groups or those with certain backgrounds and experiences have a much harder time thriving at work. In this stage, people are disengaged from the conversation around diversity and inclusion and/or uninterested in it. This resistance may be silent or public.

Unconscious bias   Social stereotypes or prejudices about certain groups that form outside your conscious awareness yet still affect how you perceive said groups.

Resources for
Inclusive Leaders

- For helpful resources and an assessment to help you determine where you are on your inclusive leader journey, please visit *inclusiveleaderthebook.com*

- This book is also available as an audio book and as an ebook. For bulk orders, please send an email to *info@jenniferbrownconsulting.com*.

- To listen to Jennifer's acclaimed podcast, search for *The Will to Change* on Apple Podcasts, Google Play, Spotify, Stitcher Radio, or your favorite podcast streaming service.

- Text "INCLUSION" to 444999 to receive a free chapter of Jennifer's first book *Inclusion: Diversity, The New Workplace and The Will to Change*.

- To find out more about Jennifer and hire her to speak at your organization, visit *jenniferbrownspeaks.com* or email *info@jenniferbrown consulting.com*.

- To learn more about Jennifer Brown Consulting's services and training programs, and to download white papers for inclusive leaders, please visit *jenniferbrownconsulting.com*.

Acknowledgments

This book is about what communities of all backgrounds can do to move the needle toward spaces of profound belonging. I am grateful for the many, many change makers, advocates, and brave voices who've inspired me to keep believing that true inclusion is a reality that we can achieve. Thank you to everyone who bought, read, and shared my first book, *Inclusion*, to every guest on and listener of my podcast, *The Will to Change*, and to every client who works with us. We are learning *with* you, every day, and together we are mighty.

Most important, though, is to say that I am humbled every day to walk this path with the Jennifer Brown Consulting team. When I founded the company, I knew right away that I didn't want to work alone on such a massive and important topic, I wanted to enable others to spread our message and to support them with whatever I could bring to the equation. I knew I'd need to convene the most talented sales and operations leadership, practitioners, project managers, researchers, and designers into a family. I also knew that this work would be difficult, requiring stamina and resilience, even on the best of days. We would need to do it together, even if we had to settle for "virtual" togetherness and high-fiving each other in airports around the world. This connectedness would enable us to keep our energy up as well as learn from each other about what's occurring in the field, in real time. To Rob Beaven, Karen Stultz, my mentor, William Lieberman, and my incredible consulting team, I couldn't steer the ship without you. That this talented, passionate group of people has honored me with their presence and brought their knowledge and their hearts to our client work is a blessing that I am still amazed by, every day. Thank you to each of you.

Within this team, certain individuals have locked arms with me to help birth this book, in addition to their many other responsibilities. Without them, I shudder to think how long the process might have taken, or how I would have adhered to my vision and managed all that goes into the creation of a book behind the scenes. They held my hand, heart, and spirit as I tried to write as brave and truthful a book as I could. To Nikki Groom, our director of marketing and my writing alter-ego, who never fails to capture my voice in uncanny ways; to Matt Luginbuhl, who managed more editorial feedback than one person should ever attempt; to Andrius Alvarez-Backus and Sidney Switzer, who could chase any research and format any footnote correctly; to Amelia Forczak, who edited and brought her ally lens to our concepts, ensuring we made our points concisely and clearly; to Doug Foresta, my producer on *The Will to Change* podcast, who has been a delight to collaborate on almost a hundred episodes that have inspired so many ideas in the book; to our book assessment design team Diane Colomer-Cheadle, Jeff Brandi, Wendy Collins, and Lena Beaven, each of whom instinctively knows how to bring ideas to life; and finally, to Veronica Pirillo, who has somehow kept our flow of events, keynotes, and conferences moving betwixt and between book activities—she is my seamless, calm, and brilliant right hand (who's made me the envy of every leader I know).

We were also the fortunate recipients of much feedback on the manuscript. Some might say we solicited more than we could act on, but there is a larger intention afoot, to carry all of those gifts, insights, and yes, challenges and cautions, forward as we move through this new phase. Our publishers' talented external reviewers went line by line through my writing in many cases, helping me capture the nuances of what can be a delicate topic. We also conducted many helpful interviews, with thought leaders and trusted experts such as Matt Wallaert, Natasha Green, Josh Stewart, Grace Figueredo, Jorge Quezada, Vinay Kapoor, Kendra Clarke, Josh Copus, Lisa Fain, Jonamay Lambert, Deb Dagit, Adam Quinton, Damon Hart, and Aimee Broadhurst. And finally, a sincere thank you to each friend and colleague who made the time to go through the manuscript, including Bob Gower, Guido Tamborini, Jane Switzer, Aditi Dussault, David Allyn, Ellyn Kerr, Jared Karol, Steve Disselhorst, Eduardo Placer, Christopher McCormick, Steve Andersen, Eric Ratinoff, Kat Gordon, Fen Bowen, and Sean Harvey.

I only wish these pages had more room to feature all your stories and insights, but never fear, there is much more to come.

It has been a delight to work with Steve Piersanti, my editor at Berrett-Koehler, who was inspired by my message and saw its importance within the pantheon of leadership and diversity books already on their bursting shelves. Steve, you have taught us so much about what constitutes a timeless book that speaks directly to the audience with respect and clarity. We are also grateful for Jeevan Sivasubramaniam, who managed the coordination of a massive amount of editorial feedback that really, in my mind, differentiates BK in terms of how it supports its authors, all with aplomb and a great sense of humor.

To my family, thank you for the unconditional support and the love you've shown me for so many years. It has been a rare blessing to have two sisters whose company I happily seek. To my parents in particular, I appreciate every day the means I was fortunate enough to be born into, which meant that I would be as prepared and equipped as I could be to communicate my message far and wide, and to get up on stage after stage, fearlessly and with joy.

Index

About the Author

Jennifer Brown is an award-winning entrepreneur, speaker, diversity and inclusion consultant, and author. Her work in talent management, human capital, and intersectional theory has redefined the boundaries of talent potential and company culture. Her bestselling book, *Inclusion: Diversity, the New Workplace and the Will to Change,* creates the case for leaders to embrace the opportunity that diversity represents, for their own growth and for the success of their organizations.

Jennifer is the host of the popular weekly podcast, *The Will to Change,* which uncovers true stories of diversity and inclusion. The podcast receives thousands of downloads each month and has featured multiple notable guests including New York Times bestselling author Sally Hogshead; ex-NFL player, advisor, and consultant Wade Davis; Priya Parker, facilitator and author of *The Art of Gathering: How We Meet and Why It Matters;* and theoretical neuroscientist Dr. Vivienne Ming.

As the founder, president, and CEO of Jennifer Brown Consulting (JBC), Jennifer's workplace strategies have been employed by some of the world's biggest companies and nonprofits in order to help employees feel like they belong and can bring their full selves to work. As a successful LGBT entrepreneur, Jennifer has been featured in media such as *The New York Times, The Wall Street Journal, Harvard Business Review, AdWeek, Bloomberg Businessweek, Forbes, Inc., CBS,* and many more.

Jennifer has spoken at many top conferences and events such as the International Diversity Forum, the Global D&I Summit, the Forum for Workplace Inclusion, the NGLCC International Business & Leadership Conference, the Out & Equal Workplace Summit, Emerging Women, SHE Summit, Responsive, the Better Man Conference, INBOUND, Interbrand's Best Global Brands event, as well as at organizations such as Allstate, Pepsico, the Bill and Melinda Gates Foundation, the NBA, Google, IBM, and many more.

In the past several years, Brown has been named Woman of the Year by Pace University, Social Entrepreneur of the year by the NYC National Association of Women Business Owners (NAWBO), a finalist for the Wells Fargo Business Owner of the Year Award, a finalist for Ernst & Young's Winning Women Program, one of the Top 40 Outstanding Women by Stonewall Community Foundation, and NYC Controller Bill Thompson's LGBT Business Owner of the Year.

About Jennifer Brown Consulting

J ennifer Brown Consulting (JBC) believes in unleashing the power of human potential, embracing diversity, and helping people—and organizations—thrive. The company is on a mission to set a new tone for business, and the world, and to create a more inclusive reality for generations to come by helping organizations create the type of workplace where people no longer feel pressure to downplay aspects of their identity in order to survive; instead, they begin to feel free to bring their full selves to work and motivated to contribute in a way that fuels bottom line growth.

As a certified woman- and LGBT-owned strategic leadership and diversity consulting firm, JBC understands how important it is to empower leaders to drive positive organizational change and the future of work in today's rapidly changing business landscape. Based in New York City with a global presence, JBC partners with HR, talent management, diversity and inclusion, and business leadership teams on change management efforts relating to human capital everywhere from North America to Southeast Asia.

Whether JBC is building classroom training on unconscious bias, setting up a diversity council, leveraging its proprietary ERG Progress Model^{SM} to transform resource groups into true business partners, launching an executive learning curriculum, rolling out a diverse talent program for an entire organization, or providing eLearning training, everything is customized to resolve each client's unique challenges.

Past clients include Walmart, Starbucks, Toyota Financial Services, Microsoft, the City of New York, T-Mobile, and many others, from the Fortune 1000 to government agencies and nonprofits.

JBC has worked with clients at all stages of their diversity and inclusion journey. Get in touch today to assess your readiness for change with a free consultation: visit *jenniferbrownconsulting.com* or email *info@jenniferbrownconsulting.com* and mention this book.

Dear reader,

Thank you for picking up this book and welcome to the worldwide BK community! You're joining a special group of people who have come together to create positive change in their lives, organizations, and communities.

What's BK all about?

Our mission is to connect people and ideas to create a world that works for all.

Why? Our communities, organizations, and lives get bogged down by old paradigms of self-interest, exclusion, hierarchy, and privilege. But we believe that can change. That's why we seek the leading experts on these challenges—and share their actionable ideas with you.

A welcome gift

To help you get started, we'd like to offer you a **free copy** of one of our bestselling ebooks:

www.bkconnection.com/welcome

When you claim your **free ebook**, you'll also be subscribed to our blog.

Our freshest insights

Access the best new tools and ideas for leaders at all levels on our blog at ideas.bkconnection.com.

Sincerely,

Your friends at Berrett-Koehler

Certified

B

Corporation